"If you're ready to join the ranks of published writers, use *Living Write*'s powerful psychological tools to enhance your productivity and help you achieve your dreams of professional success. And if you're already published, apply Kelly L. Stone's techniques to give your success a big boost!"

—Suzanne Adair, winner of the Patrick D. Smith Literature Award from the Florida Historical Society

"This book is amazing! Every page contains solid advice, inspiring comments, and concrete steps that can get a new writer off to a great start and that keep the writer who's been slogging away motivated and enthused. I know what I'm going to gift my writer friends for their birthdays, their successes, their rejections—heck, just because they're writers!"

—Mary Buckham, coauthor of *Break Into Fiction*®: *11 Steps to Building a Story That Sells*

"Kelly L. Stone's *Living Write* is a treasure trove of riches for writers facing the challenge of achieving their goals. She combines sophisticated psychological theory with practical advice gleaned from the experiences of successful authors to help writers at any stage in their careers and her recommendations address both the daily work of writing and the big dreams. I will recommend this book to friends!"

—Katharine Ashe, author of *Swept Away by a Kiss*

the secret
to
inviting your
craft *into*
your daily
life

Living Write

the secret
to
inviting your
craft *into*
your daily
life

Living Write

Kelly L. Stone, author of *Thinking Write*

CD written and performed by R. Michael Stone, MS

adamsmedia
Avon, Massachusetts

Published by
Adams Media, a division of F+W Media, Inc.
57 Littlefield Street, Avon, MA 02322. U.S.A.
www.adamsmedia.com

ISBN 10: 1-4405-0624-8

ISBN 13: 978-1-4405-0624-6

eISBN 10: 1-4405-0866-6

eISBN 13: 978-1-4405-0866-0

Printed in the United States of America.

10   9   8   7   6   5   4   3   2   1

Library of Congress Cataloging-in-Publication Data
Stone, Kelly L.
  Living write / Kelly L. Stone.
      p. cm.
  Includes bibliographical references and index.
  ISBN-13: 978-1-4405-0624-6
  ISBN-10: 1-4405-0624-8
  ISBN-13: 978-1-4405-0866-0 (electronic)
  ISBN-10: 1-4405-0866-6 (electronic)
  1. Authorship—Psychological aspects. I. Title.
  PN171.P83.S86 2010
  808'.02—dc22
2010022576

This publication is designed to provide accurate and authoritative information
with regard to the subject matter covered. It is sold with the understanding that
the publisher is not engaged in rendering legal, accounting, or other professional
advice. If legal advice or other expert assistance is required, the services of a competent professional person should be sought.
  —From a *Declaration of Principles* jointly adopted by a Committee of the American
              Bar Association and a Committee of Publishers and Associations

Many of the designations used by manufacturers and sellers to distinguish their
product are claimed as trademarks. Where those designations appear in this book
and Adams Media was aware of a trademark claim, the designations have been
printed with initial capital letters.

Images © clipart.com

This book is available at quantity discounts for bulk purchases.
For information, please call 1-800-289-0963.

Acknowledgments

I would like to thank my publisher, Adams Media, for acquiring this book; thanks to my wonderful editor, Katie Corcoran Lytle, for championing the proposal and for support and guidance from start to finish; I'm eternally grateful to the successful authors quoted within these pages who took time away from their own deadlines to give me an interview; and thanks once again to R. Michael Stone, MS, for lending his expertise to this project through consultation on subject matter and for writing and producing a companion CD that brings to life the concepts of the book.

part iii
Deepen Your Writing

How to Become a Writer

YOU HAVE A STORY TO TELL. There is a book inside of you, dying to get out, that only you can write. You may think about writing your story down or dream about seeing your name on the spine of a novel. You ache to write. Maybe you have scribbled notes around the house, or have an unfinished manuscript languishing under your bed. You want to finish it, and yet you don't take action for any number of reasons. The act of writing seems mysterious, intimidating, daunting, and overwhelming. You don't know how to start, but at the same time you yearn to get going.

Many people think that writing is some mysterious process that has to be done in isolation, away from the day-to-day business of real life. Nothing could be further from the truth. The reality is that successful authors have found ways to bring writing into their daily lives by making it part of their regular routine. You can do this, too. You can become a writer while you parent your children, work your job, tend to your social obligations, and manage your household. To be a writer, you simply have to write. Just as you don't agonize over when you will have time to shower in the morning because taking a daily shower is habit, a writer doesn't agonize over how the one page will get written because it's habit. It's a given. It's part of the daily schedule. The shower gets taken, the teeth get brushed, and the page gets written. Making writing a daily habit might sound hard, but *Living Write* will get you on your way!

This book will also reveal the cumulative power that will build as you begin to bring writing more and more into your daily life. Daily actions create long-term outcomes. It's what you do now, here, today, that will determine if you finish your novel. The more you write, the more you will feel like writing. Momentum will build, and with it, your motivation, dedication, and enthusiasm for writing. You'll begin to tap into your subconscious riches more easily. You'll build a bridge from your subconscious to your conscious mind that will enhance your creativity. Bringing the craft of writing into your daily life *is* the key to achieving your writing dreams.

This is a phenomenon that I've witnessed firsthand. Over the years, I have had the pleasure of interviewing more than 150 successful authors, many of whom had numerous bestsellers under their belt. All of these writers had stories of incredible perseverance, drive, and persistence that propelled them forward over the course of sometimes as many as twenty years before they finally reached their long-term goals of becoming successful writers. I learned that bestselling author Steve Berry wrote eight manuscripts over twelve years and received eighty-five rejections before he sold his first novel. Allison Brennan started more than 100 manuscripts and received scathing rejections before she achieved the outstanding success she has earned today. Bestselling author Jodi Picoult kept writing her stories despite the fact that more than 100 rejection letters were delivered to her mailbox. And *New York Times* bestselling author Sherrilyn Kenyon was told that no publishing house was interested in her work and that she should stop submitting her manuscripts, prompting her to throw her typewriter into the trash can. She eventually dug it back out and went on to write the book that launched her incredible career.

Look at any successful writer and you will find some version of this story. Even writers who burst onto the scene with a book that rockets them to fame have, more likely than not, been quietly plodding along, day after day, toward a dream that sometimes felt elusive, impossible, and out of reach. And yet it wasn't. These writers succeeded because they learned to make writing an integral part of their daily lives—and because they outlined plans that drove their daily writing behaviors in predictable ways so they could achieve predictable long-term results—and you can, too.

As a licensed mental health counselor, I will teach you how to apply proven psychological techniques such as the thought-feeling-behavior cycle and other tools so that you can more easily incorporate writing into your daily life. You will learn about role-modeling, Image Incorporation, and using "Writing Counselors" to communicate with your subconscious mind. These techniques are designed to bring about daily writing results and will keep you striving toward your writing dreams.

Each chapter has an activity that I encourage you to complete; these practical and easy-to-use exercises will help you implement the ideas presented in the chapter. Because the activities build on each other, you will want to purchase either a journal or a spiral notebook and use it to record your exercises. In the final chapter, all the activities are grouped together into a 21-day program with suggested time frames for completion. The benefit of doing all of the activities in twenty-one days is that you will begin to bring an intense focus on writing and achieving your writing goals into your day-to-day awareness. This focus will bolster your efforts at making daily writing a habit in your life and will establish a foundation on which you can move forward. However, you can also choose to complete the activities as you read along and then review, tweak, or re-do them in the suggested 21-day format when you get to the final chapter. That approach is beneficial as well and will add the impact of repetition to your exercises.

There is also an accompanying CD with four tracks that provides guided exercises to assist you in learning how to apply some of the techniques that we will discuss. For optimal results, I suggest you read the chapter first before using the exercises on the CD. A small digital recorder or tape recorder will come in handy, too, since the tracks allow you to personalize the exercises with your own material for optimal results.

Used together, the activities and CD are powerful tools that will help you take charge of your daily writing life, your thought-feeling-behavior cycle, your writing habits, and your long-range writing endeavors so that you can achieve goal-directed results.

You can be the writer that you want to be. It's as simple as opening the door and inviting writing into your daily life. I know you can do it. I believe in you.

Let's get started.

part i

Inviting Writing into Your Daily Life

In this first part, we will discuss myriad ways in which you can invite the craft of writing into your daily life. This practice starts, simply enough, with writing every day. You may not realize it, but whether or not you write today is important—it matters. There is power in the act of daily writing, and when you touch your craft every day, it becomes part of your life, a habit that you'll miss if you skip it too often. Successful writers have learned to weave the craft of writing into their daily lives—and now, you can, too.

Chapter 1

The *Power*

of Daily

Writing

SUCCESS IN ANY ENDEAVOR CAN BE PREDICTED based on how a person thinks, feels, and behaves toward her goals. A person who has success-oriented thoughts and who feels confident in her abilities will naturally take daily actions that bring about her desired outcomes. She will feel enthusiastic, motivated, and dedicated to those outcomes because she thinks, feels, and acts her way toward reaching them, and she does the things every day necessary to achieve success.

This is the case with writing, too. An aspiring author who thinks positive thoughts and believes in herself will touch her craft daily, which will generate the enthusiasm and motivation to set goals. She will then cultivate the dedication required to take steps to reach those goals over a long period of time. She will write every day or take action every day toward her writing dream. She will act in methodical, self-disciplined ways that bring about her desired outcomes. She will think, feel, and act in ways that stimulate enthusiasm, motivation, and dedication for achieving success as a writer as she defines it.

You can be that writer. There are ways for you to create or re-establish patterns in your life that will direct your energies toward writing success. Even if you have gotten off track with your efforts to become a successful writer, it's never too late to start again. You can learn to generate the enthusiasm, motivation, and dedication needed to work toward your long-term writing goals on a daily basis by directing your thought-feeling-behavior cycle in positive, goal-oriented ways. You can create for yourself what is known in psychology as a positive self-fulfilling prophecy, which is a belief system that sets you up to succeed.

We will discuss the thought-feeling-behavior cycle later in this chapter. But first, let's take a look at the importance of enthusiasm, motivation, and dedication for bringing more writing into your life.

Where Do Enthusiasm, Motivation, and Dedication Come From?

Napoleon Hill, the founder of modern day positive-thinking techniques, once wrote that the true meaning of life could be found in the struggle to reach a goal that was always in the future. Once that goal is reached, another goal emerges—again in the future—that you then set your sights on achieving. Because of this dynamic, happiness, like the goal itself, is always just beyond reach. Hill concluded that because of the nature of achievement, personal fulfillment lies not in the attainment of a goal but in the *striving* to attain it.

Becoming a writer works in much the same way. When you first start out on your journey, your first goal is to simply find time to write. You hash out a schedule, shove aside all distractions, and finally meet your goal of writing every day. Then a new goal comes up: finish your novel. After a year or two of struggling to overcome various obstacles, you finally finish your book, only to see yet a third goal emerge: find an agent. You take the bull by the horns and spend some time landing an agent, and now the goal becomes getting the novel published *while* writing another novel. And on it goes. The attainment of each goal brings momentary satisfaction and the realization that another, higher goal has now taken its place. The process of achieving your ultimate writing goal, which I call your Vision of Success, is always the dream at your fingertips, the dream you are always chasing, the light that shines in your future. Pursuing a future goal helps create enthusiasm, motivation, and dedication now, in the present, to pursue it and, for writers, the act of daily writing brings the happiness and fulfillment that will fuel your dedication to your craft.

Traits That Contribute to Enthusiasm, Motivation, and Dedication

The writing process personifies the struggle of setting and attaining goals. Ironically, it is out of this struggle that you will be able to form the ability to generate enthusiasm, motivation, and dedication to your long-term writing goals. I have seen this phenomenon in action. Over the past three years, I have interviewed approximately 150 successful and bestselling authors while conducting research for my books. No matter the genre, I discovered that there were key traits that contributed to these writers' successes. These traits include:

- *Dedication*: successful writers possess intense dedication to pursue their objectives despite all obstacles and in the absence of external signs of progress.
- *Deliberate thought patterns*: successful writers form habitual thought patterns that are goal-oriented, future-focused, and allow no room for the idea of failure.
- *Motivation*: successful writers are motivated by the act of writing.
- *Enthusiasm*: successful writers possess enthusiasm for writing that springs from the actual act of writing.
- *Discipline*: successful writers have the ability to consistently exercise self-discipline. Most write every day whether they feel like it or not.

- *Confidence*: successful writers develop a deep confidence in themselves and their abilities as writers, and they have acquired the ability to quickly refocus when this confidence is shaken.

New York Times bestselling author Dianna Love, author of *Silent Truth* and other novels, demonstrates how these traits can lead an author to strive for success over many years and through many unforeseen obstacles. Love says, "My long-term goal was to write and publish fiction. After selling my first book to a major publisher, a book that won nine awards and sold out in the first month, I did not get another contract for three years. I had a change in editors and nothing I submitted resonated. The one thing I did do was to continue writing and working to hone my craft. I continued to speak at conferences and reader events during my involuntary hiatus from being published so when I had a new book out the readers still knew my name. I stayed on my original path and just worked harder to reach that next level." Notice how Love continued to focus her daily actions on her desired outcomes, even when there was no obvious progress toward the goal? This is a good example of how daily writing fuels the thoughts, feelings, and behaviors that lead to success.

The Burning Desire to Write

In addition to these traits, another common thread among authors is that they write because they must, not because they want or have to. While a looming deadline creates a great deal of initiative to complete a project, the underlying idea is that writing is a labor of love. It's something that the majority of writers want to be doing all of the time. I call this compulsion the Burning Desire to Write. It's that feeling that you can't *not* write. You, as an aspiring author, also possess the Burning Desire to Write or you would not be reading this book.

This Burning Desire to Write is an important aspect of what will get you to your desk every day. Indeed, Napoleon Hill states that your ability to achieve anything has to start with desire. The Burning Desire to Write is the foundation of all writing success; it's the starting point. In the simplest of terms, enthusiasm, motivation, and dedication spring from the Burning Desire to Write. However, desire alone is not adequate to create results. In order to achieve your objectives, you have to create plans and take actions every day. You have to set goals. You have to visualize yourself succeeding. You have to anticipate that there will be obstacles along the way and make a plan for overcoming them. You have to do something every day toward your dream. Desire is the foundation, but in order to actually get the results and the outcomes that you want (e.g., success as a writer), you must use your thoughts, feelings, and behaviors to bring the craft of writing into your daily life.

The Write Stuff

"The more I write, the more I feel like writing."

—Novelist Cynthia Eden

The Thought-Feeling-Behavior Cycle

Enthusiasm, motivation, and dedication are necessary for your success as a writer. If you're worried that you don't have these emotional tools, don't worry—they can be learned as part of the *thought-feeling-behavior* cycle. This cycle is a well-documented psychological principle; it states that how you think and feel guides your behavior, and also that how you behave can actually change your thoughts and feelings. But, this powerful principle also asserts that you can act your way into feeling and thinking certain things, which is especially helpful to a writer who feels she has lost her way.

This circular, interrelated loop of the thought-feeling-behavior cycle is important to note. What this means is that, when you change one element of the cycle, you will by necessity change the other two. This dynamic makes the system very useful for writers because if one element is easier for you to work with than the other two, you can focus on that one element to achieve your writing success. For example, if it's easier for you to change your thoughts than your behaviors, you can focus on and strengthen the thought element of the cycle when using the techniques in this book. If it's easier for you to change your actions, you can take that route. Despite the fact that this is a simple, straightforward process, it's still very effective: working with your thought-feeling-behavior cycle will help you make significant strides with your writing goals.

Let's take a look at each of three elements individually.

Thoughts

Whether you are aware of it or not, you have a constant inner dialogue going on inside your head. Even when you are engaged in conversation with another person, watching a movie, or attending a meeting at work, there is a subtext of running commentary going on inside you.

Often you are not aware of this running commentary because much of it occurs on a subconscious level. But this subconscious dialogue is usually what impacts your feelings and behavior the most. With practice, you can begin to notice these thoughts and gain some insight into how they are affecting the way you feel and how you behave. For example, you might attend a writing conference and overhear another aspiring author tell someone that the editor to whome she pitched her manuscript asked to see the first three chapters of the book. If you are not feeling particularly enthusiastic about your own work-in-progress, you might have an immediate negative thought about your upcoming pitch session, such as "that probably won't happen to me" or something along those lines. That thought might zip across your mind at a sub-conscious level, but it would create certain feelings and behaviors that would likely sabotage your pitch session. Learning to identify these types of thoughts is important for controlling your thought-feeling-behavior cycle, and you will learn how to do this with the techniques in this book.

The Write Stuff

"I stayed on my original path and just worked harder to reach that next level."

—*New York Times* bestselling author Dianna Love

Feelings

Continuing with the example above, the feelings associated with the thought "that probably won't happen to me" can range from anger to disappointment to sadness. This feeling would likely produce more thoughts that are counter-productive. An important component of feelings is that they are highly suscep-tible to your thoughts and your chronic thinking patterns. Over time, chronic thought patterns program the subconscious mind to bring about a reality that reinforces those feelings. In psychology, this is called a self-fulfilling prophecy, which I mentioned ear-lier. It means that because you believe something at a deep level, whether it's true or not, eventually your thoughts and feelings program your subconscious to create that reality.

The good news is that how you feel is subject to your thoughts. For example, a common technique for helping people to feel bet-ter about themselves and improve their lives is to have them sim-ply say that they feel good out loud several times every day. In one study, the French psychologist Emile Coué asked patients receiving services in a hospital for various mental health issues to say, "Every day in every way, I'm getting better and better" over and over. Eventually these people improved regardless of the treatment protocol that they received, and regardless of what their diagnosis was. This is because whenever a person is thinking and saying that he feels good, he starts to feel that way even if there is no change in their external circumstances. These feelings then influence his thoughts and behaviors.

You can try this for yourself by conducting this simple experiment. The next time you find yourself in a bad mood, say out loud, repeatedly, "I'm in a wonderful mood." Observe how long it takes until your feelings begin to change.

Use this exercise to bring writing into your daily life. Every morning when you wake up, say out loud, "I feel like writing today." Keep saying it until you really do feel like writing.

Behaviors

Behaviors are direct manifestations of thoughts and feelings. It's easy to see how using the example above. When the writer thinks that the editor at his pitch session will not ask for his manuscript, he feels prematurely rejected. How do you think this will affect his behavior at the actual appointment? Will he walk in with his shoulders squared and head held high? It's unlikely. Will this writer return home feeling inspired to keep chipping away at his work-in-progress? Probably not.

However, if the thoughts and feelings about the upcoming pitch session are positive, the writer will walk in exuding a positive attitude, which will then influence the session. For example, say the writer had overheard the comment from the other aspiring author and thought, "I bet my editor asks to see my manuscript, too." His feelings would have immediately been buoyed up; he would have felt confident and eager to get to his appointment. When the time arrived, he would have walked up to the editor with a smile on his face and a spring in his step. He would have exuded confidence, which may have affected the result of his pitch session. Back at home, his behaviors would have reflected a writer who thought and felt positively about his abilities and his chances of finding success as a writer—in other words, he would have continued working every day on his work-in-progress regardless of the outcome of the pitch session.

How Can You Take Control?

You can see how thoughts, feelings, and behaviors are directly connected. This is why learning to control your thought-feeling-behavior cycle is so important—because it's cumulative and self-perpetuating. Let me give you an example of how you can take advantage of this thought-feeling-behavior cycle.

Daily Direction

Use the energy of resistance to your advantage. When you don't feel like writing, instead of thinking about how much you don't want to write, pull out your journal and write about why you don't feel like writing instead. When you are finished, move directly to your work-in-progress and write at least one page.

Change Thoughts to Change Feelings

Let's say you have as a daily goal to write 1,000 words. When the time arrives for you to get to your desk, how you think and feel about that goal will dictate whether or not you follow through. If you think positive thoughts and have feelings of enthusiasm about your writing and your writing abilities, you will naturally behave in ways that will get those 1,000 words written. If you do not have positive thoughts and feelings toward your writing, you probably won't sit down to write—or if you do, you may be unable to produce your word count goal. This is not to say that there won't be times when you do not feel like writing, because all writers have days like that, but the key lies in what you tell yourself about how you're feeling. If you allow your thoughts of not wanting to write to negatively influence your actions, you probably won't write. For example, if you start thinking, "What's the use, I'll never get published anyway," or "It's taking too long to write this book, so why bother," then the thought of not wanting to write will create feelings that impact your behavior in a negative way; you may choose to watch television instead of sitting down to write.

But by changing your thought-feeling-behavior cycle, you will be able to change one element of the cycle and produce results. Let's say you don't feel like writing but still want to fulfill your daily writing schedule. One way to achieve success here is by choosing to change your thoughts about the day's work. You can do this by thinking or saying to yourself that you cleared this time on your schedule to write and therefore need to sit down and write; you can tell yourself that successful writers write and that you will one day be a successful writer, too, and so on. These thoughts will influence your feelings toward writing—you will probably feel less negative about the writing than you did before you changed your thoughts—and your resulting behavior will be to go to the desk and begin writing.

A critical point to notice here is that once you begin writing, your feelings will *keep changing*, and you will become increasingly more positive about the writing process. In fact, a common phenomenon for many writers is that inspiration to write appears only after they have taken the necessary steps to begin the day's work. So keep at it!

Changing Behavior First

For some people, it's easier to change their actions than it is to try to think or feel differently. Behavior is a powerful statement to your subconscious mind; when you act in certain ways—whether you feel like it or not—over time you program your subconscious mind to believe that you are capable of that behavior on a consistent basis.

You have probably heard the saying "fake it 'til you make it." Similarly, in many self-help groups, the advice "take the action and the insight will follow" is commonly given. What these phrases mean is that you can act (behave) your way into doing something until your thoughts and feelings catch up. So changing the element of behavior changes the other two elements of thought and feeling and creates results.

Using the above example, you would exercise self-discipline and get to your desk and begin writing, despite how you may be feeling or thinking. The act of writing will then change your thoughts and feelings in positive, goal directed ways that result in written pages.

Programming Your Subconscious

Chronic thoughts, feelings, and behaviors create the results you are visualizing by programming your subconscious mind to bring those results into reality. In the simplest of terms, it works this way because the things you do, think, and feel all the time train your subconscious mind to certain outcomes according to what you are doing, thinking, and feeling. It's that self-fulfilling prophecy that I mentioned above. You expect a certain outcome—positive or negative—and then think, feel, and act in ways that program your subconscious to bring that outcome to pass.

For example, you make the choice every day between writing or not writing; if you write every day, the pages begin to stack up, and in a relatively short amount of time you have a finished product. But if you make the choice not to write more days out of the week, that means that you are chronically wishing that you could be a writer but it does not bring about a finished book, article, or essay.

Your thought-feeling-behavior cycle is an important part of your success as a writer because it drives your daily actions, which are critical to your long-term results. The good news is that you can get your results entirely under your command. The activity below will give you the opportunity to look at your current cycle, see the self-fulfilling prophecy you are operating under, and make adjustments as needed to improve your chances of writing success.

Activity: Get Ready to Write!

The first track on the CD is designed to help you have a successful writing session. You may use it at any time and as often as you wish. For this exercise, as with all of the CD exercises, find a comfortable place where you will not be disturbed for about twenty to thirty minutes. Lower the lights, turn off your cell phone, and get into a comfortable position. Move directly from the CD exercise into a writing session.

Activity: Determine Your Thought-Feeling-Behavior Cycle

To determine your current thought-feeling-behavior cycle and self-fulfilling prophecy, you need to identify your thoughts, feelings, and behaviors related to writing. For one week, record in your notebook everything that you think, feel, and do related to writing. Make three columns on a page and label them thoughts, feelings, and behaviors, and include a place for the date. You will need to carry your notebook with you all the time to ensure that you will capture as much material as possible.

You want to capture all the statements—both positive and negative—that you catch yourself saying or thinking about your writing abilities or your writing future, any feelings of wanting to write or not wanting to write, feeling frustrated with your writing, feeling encouraged with it, and so forth. It's especially important to note your thoughts and feelings during times when you are in the act of writing, supposed to be writing, reading of another writer's success, reading a craft book, and so forth. These situations will trigger your thoughts related to your own writing and abilities.

As you complete this activity, be alert to the thought-feeling-behavior cycle. When you capture your thoughts, immediately write down one or two feelings that are associated with that thought. Remember, thoughts *always* create feelings. Lastly, record how these thoughts and feelings impact your behavior. You may discover a lack of confidence in your writing abilities, which leads you to skip your daily writing schedule. Maybe you accidentally forget to mail out that query letter? You decide not to enter a contest or you miss the deadline for entry. Make a note of all of these behaviors.

Other ways that a negative thought-feeling cycle can impact behavior includes not applying yourself to your writing projects like you know you should. Maybe you are not taking advantage of a local writer's group or attending conferences and workshops to improve your skills. Those are the sorts of behaviors that occur from a negative thought-feeling cycle.

At the end of one week, look at your list and identify the areas that are problematic for you. It's likely that you will notice which element of the thought-feeling-behavior cycle is more influential for you than the others. You may be someone who notices feelings first, then thoughts and behaviors. Or you may notice behaviors first and have to ferret out the thoughts behind those behaviors. That's okay. Simply note patterns and themes to your own cycle and spot trouble areas.

Next, in a separate column create a replacement thought to any negative thought, a replacement feeling for any problem feeling, and a replacement behavior for any problem behavior. Your chart should look something like this in your notebook:

Date: 5/25

Thought, Feeling, Behavior	Replacement Thoughts, Feelings, or Behaviors
I'll never make it as a writer	I'll make it as a writer
discouraged	encouraged
skipping writing schedule	work a writing schedule

Identify at least two problem areas that you will work on for the remainder of the time you are reading this book. You may want to write your replacements on index cards and keep them with you at all times.

Example of Replacement Thoughts, Feelings, and Behaviors in Action

Let me give you an example of how this chart can work for you. Let's say that you set aside time each evening to write but every time it rolls around, you discover that you are not, in fact, going to your desk to write. Since you are doing this exercise, you stop and notice that you are not writing. You identify the thought associated with your lack of writing. This might be something like "I don't feel like pushing myself to write," which speaks to motivation, or "I wrote last week, so I deserve to take a week off," which speaks to dedication, or "I'll never finish that novel, so why bother," which is a direct result of a lack of enthusiasm. The corresponding feelings that these thoughts cause might be a sense of dispiritedness, feeling like a failure, or lack of esteem for yourself for failing to follow through with your writing schedule. The obvious behavioral manifestation of these thoughts and feelings is that you do not follow through with your writing schedule.

If this happens once a year, it's not a problem, but when it becomes a pattern that results in consistently missed writing appointments, then the writing does not get done, which eliminates any possibility of success. Do you see how this creates a negative self-fulfilling prophecy by setting you up for failure?

To turn this negative thought-feeling-behavior cycle around, the replacement thought for "I'll never finish that novel, so why bother" can become "All books are written one page at a time." The replacement feeling for the dispiritedness becomes a sense of empowerment and motivation. The corresponding behavior changes from avoiding writing to going to the desk and fulfilling the writing schedule. This is how you take control of your thought-feeling-behavior cycle.

Live Your Life Write

Never forget how important daily writing is to your success! The thought-feeling-behavior cycle determines your daily writing actions, and your daily actions determine your long-term results. There are simple ways to take charge of your thought-feeling-behavior cycle so that you can bring more writing into your daily life. Remember:

- Your Burning Desire to Write is the foundation of your writing success, but desire alone is not adequate to create results. You must also take action by writing every day.
- The thought-feeling-behavior cycle is circular and inter-related. When you affect one element, you automatically affect the other two.
- Learning to use replacement thoughts, feelings, and behaviors is one way to take control of your thought-feeling-behavior cycle and create a positive self-fulfilling prophecy.

Chapter 2

Your *Writer* Self-Image

A POSITIVE IMAGE OF YOURSELF AS A WRITER is essential to bringing the craft of writing into your daily life. Why? Because the writer who has a positive image of himself makes writing a habit; he believes himself to be a writer instead of someone who casually sits down to write only when the mood strikes. Your Writer Self-Image is based on your thoughts, feelings, and behaviors, which determine the day-to-day beliefs and actions under which you as an aspiring writer operate as you move toward meeting your goals. Your Writer Self-Image is a reflection of your self-fulfilling prophecy, and it influences the amount of enthusiasm, motivation, and dedication you have toward meeting your writing goals.

The writer who exudes self-confidence in his abilities and his work, who harbors a positive anticipation of the future of his writing career, and who eagerly forges ahead toward his long-term writing goals is the writer who will most likely succeed in meeting those goals, whatever they may be. To create a successful Writer Self-Image, you have to behave like a writer by writing or taking some action toward your writing dream every day.

So how can you develop a successful Writer Self-Image so that you can bring writing into your daily life? How can you find the enthusiasm, motivation, and dedication to write every day, and how you can use those reasons to impact your thought-feeling-behavior cycle in a positive way? Let's find out!

What Is *Your* Writer Self-Image?

In many ways, your Writer Self-Image is like a blueprint; it's a big picture that outlines your potential accomplishments and successes as well as pinpoints areas where you need improvement or shoring up. It's a collection of traits that you either possess or want to develop. In general, your self-image consists of the following:

- how you think about yourself
- how you think about your abilities
- how you think about your past accomplishments and mistakes
- where you see yourself going in the future
- your deeply held convictions about your levels of competence to attain the goals you have set for yourself in life

Your Writer Self-Image is clearly based on thoughts, feelings, and behaviors that are characteristic of you as an author. How you think and feel about yourself as a writer will influence your behaviors and, since the cycle is circular, how you behave toward your writing goals will also influence how you think and feel about them. You can also think of your self-image is as collection of attributes, traits, and values. These characteristics dictate how you think, feel, and behave on a daily basis, and over time, create your outcomes. If there are certain desirable qualities of a writer that you currently do not have, you can develop them within yourself using the techniques in this book.

Let's look at each of these Writer Self-Image components.

The Write Stuff

"Writing can be rewarding in many ways. Contemplate what it is that most satisfies you, and embrace it."

—Novelist Nancy Martin

Attributes and Traits

Attributes and traits are the desirable qualities that make up who you are as a writer, distinguishing characteristics that define you, and the unique stamp that you put on your writing and your writing life. Examples of attributes and traits include being:

- disciplined
- motivated
- inspired
- hard-working
- persistent
- positive
- confident

You may have desired attributes and traits that are not listed here. Give some thought to the qualities that define who you are as a writer. At the end of the chapter, you will have the opportunity to use these to define your Writer Self-Image.

Values

Values are standards or principles that you consider important. For the writer, values represent deeply held personal convictions about why you want to write, and they can often be found in the emotional reasons why you want to achieve your writing goals, which you will have the opportunity to define at the end of this chapter. Values typically meet a personal need and include such things as gaining recognition, leaving behind a legacy, earning a sense of accomplishment, meeting a challenge, and so on.

There are many reasons why people write. Channeling negative emotions into something productive is why bestselling author CJ Lyons, a medical doctor and author of *Lifelines* and other medical thrillers, began writing. "During my pediatric internship a very close friend, one of my fellow interns was murdered," she says. "I turned to my writing to find my way out of my grief and despair."

Others value the act of sharing that writing allows them to do; it helps them bring their stories to the world. "I write for people who like to read the same things that I like to read, so in that way, I'm always writing for myself," says Alan Bradley, author of *The Sweetness at the Bottom of the Pie*.

Some writers want to leave a legacy for their families and value the ability to act as historians for their lives and times. Others want to make their mark on the world by getting their signature novel out of their heads and onto the bookshelves. You may feel that the story you have to tell will make a contribution to society in some way. Personally, I write because of the deep satisfaction that comes from working toward my goals every day. When I meet my daily wordcount goal, I feel like I'm living up to the high standards that I set for myself. Working on my goals every day adds meaning to my life. Maybe you feel this way, too. But whatever your reason for writing, whatever your *why*, the emotions underlying that why are integral to your Writer Self-Image.

Why a Positive Writer Self-Image Is Important

When it comes to success, self-image can make or break you. A positive Writer Self-Image motivates you to write every day, helps you devote yourself to a writing schedule, and aids you in working every day toward your writing goals. If publication is your goal, a positive Writer Self-Image provides you with the belief in yourself that you need to submit your work, handle rejection successfully, and persist until your goal is reached. If penning poetry is your aim, a positive Writer Self-Image helps you believe that your craft is worthy of your time, gives you the internal encouragement to put those words on paper, and allows you to cherish the work you are creating. In all cases, a positive Writer Self-Image builds up your self-esteem through successful completion of the creative act.

The Write Stuff

"I'm always writing for myself."

—Novelist Alan Bradley

Your Writer Self-Image is under your power and control. It starts with subconscious beliefs—your deep-seated feelings related to yourself, your writing, and your abilities as a writer—and winds out into your daily thoughts. These thoughts, when positive and goal-oriented, spur daily actions that help you meet your goals, and you will begin to think, act, and feel like a writer. And when you feel like a writer, you will write. When you believe that you are a writer, you will write. When you have a solid Writer Self-Image, bringing the craft of writing into your daily routine will become as natural to you as sleeping because it will be a part of who you are.

Your Writer Self-Image Is Constant

While emotions are fleeting, meaning that they can change minute-to-minute or even second-to-second, your Writer Self-Image is a more constant state of mind that is linked to your subconscious belief system. This belief system is based on the years of programming that you have been doing with your thought-feeling-behavior cycle. For instance, if you have spent years writing but have not gathered the courage to send out your work because you fear rejection, you may have programmed that fear into your subconscious mind by thinking thoughts like, "Why send this out? No one will take it anyway" or something to that effect. Those types of statements, and the corresponding feelings of discouragement, fear, lack of confidence, and so forth, eventually become part of your Writer Self-Image. Clearly this is not the type of Writer Self-Image you want, but it is possible to create a more positive and proactive one with the exercises found later on in this chapter.

Your Writer Self-Image Helps You Weather the Storms of the Journey

A positive Writer Self-Image can help you navigate the difficult periods that all writers go through at every stage of their careers. Even writers with very strong, positive Writer Self-Images have periods of doubt or frustration. Over the course of the many years it can take to become successful, it's natural to have high and low points. However, a person with a positive Writer Self-Image copes with doubt and frustration in fundamentally different ways than someone with a negative self-image. The attributes, traits, and values of a positive Writer Self-Image create a foundation upon which you can stand as you move ahead on your journey. A positive Writer Self-Image helps you take rejection less personally—or not personally at all. It helps you get back in the saddle more quickly and helps you move ahead with your own objectives again. It also helps you to overcome any obstacle standing in your way of obtaining the success that you desire. A positive Writer Self-Image keeps you writing every day because that's what writers do—*they write*.

Novelist Lori Foster, author of *Back in Black* and other novels, explains that when she first began writing, she saw herself as someone who was going to eventually succeed. "I'm not a person who takes failure lightly," she says. "When I decide to do something, I do my very best." This positive attitude was part of Foster's Writer Self-Image. It motivated her to start writing and keep striving toward getting published, despite receiving rejections for five years and writing ten unpublished manuscripts.

You can do this, too. Developing a positive Writer Self-Image is a creative act in and of itself, and it is a process that is constantly evolving. As you earn accomplishments, your positive self-image spirals upward to a higher point. This higher level contains additional challenges that allow you to stretch out of your comfort zone and achieve even greater heights.

Your Writer Self-Image Gives You a Sense of Purpose

A Writer Self-Image gives you a reason to pursue your writing goals. It also gives you a sense of purpose, which is what will get you to your desk in the years to come. This purpose does not have to be lofty. Maybe you discover that your Writer Self-Image simply adds value to your life by helping you pursue a goal to your desired outcome. That's fine. As I mentioned above, I write because working every day toward my writing goals adds meaning to my life. When I don't write, I get agitated, bored, and irritable. That reason alone is enough of a purpose to get me to the desk.

Your Writer Self-Image Helps You Advance Your Goals

Writers with a positive self-image approach obstacles differently that those with a negative self-image. Let's take rejection as an example. Say a writer pitches his nonfiction book to an editor at a conference. The editor tells him at the end of his ten minutes that the project does not suit her needs at this time and declines to look at the manuscript. He thanks her for her time and leaves the pitch session.

An aspiring author with a negative self-image would allow the editor's rejection to reinforce his already existing negative thoughts, feelings, and behaviors. It might cause thoughts like, "I knew she was going to hate my idea" or "I'm never going to sell this book." This in turn might trigger feelings of hopelessness and even embarrassment. These feelings would then influence the writer's behavior for the remainder of the day—he might not attend workshops that would be useful to his fledgling career. Back at home he might abandon his writing schedule.

Daily Direction

If distractions like the Internet or e-mail pull you away from your writing, invest in a laptop or an AlphaSmart and use it only for writing.

On the flip side, the aspiring author with a positive Writer Self-Image would take the rejection in stride. He would have thoughts like, "It only takes one yes to get published" or "My idea isn't suitable for that one editor." Momentary disappointment would, on the heels of thoughts like this, morph into feelings of determination to find an editor who is interested in the project and willing to take it on. These feelings would produce behaviors consistent with the persistence needed to meet long-term writing goals; the writer would attend workshops, learn new skills, and network with other writers. Back at home he would double his efforts at becoming successful. With a positive Writer Self-Image and a positive self-fulfilling prophecy, rejection and other setbacks are not devastating but rather inspire more action toward becoming successful.

Developing a Positive Writer Self-Image

So how do you develop a positive Writer Self-Image? The first strategy is to believe you are a writer. Say it out loud: *I am a writer*. Then begin to think of yourself as a writer, and do so at every opportunity. Then begin to act like a writer. What do writers do? They write every day.

Another way to develop a positive Writer Self-Image is to pinpoint the attributes, traits, and values that define you as an author. These attributes, traits, and values are often discovered when you begin to understand the reasons why you want to be a successful author. What is the driving force behind your urge to set words on paper?

As I mentioned earlier, the *why* of why you write is often where you can find the attributes, traits, and values that make up your Writer Self-Image. You begin learning what qualities are important to you about you as a writer by listing all the reasons why you want to write and become a successful writer, however you define it. The reasons why you want to achieve a goal are just as important as the goal itself. The *emotional* component of a goal is what inspires the thoughts, feelings, and behaviors to pursue it—what will it mean for you when you achieve the goal? That's the important piece.

For instance, maybe becoming a successful writer means that you can work less and spend more time with your kids. The emotional component of that goal is that you can spend more time with your family, and a value of this Writer Self-Image might be "lives a balanced life." That "why" generates enthusiasm and motivation about the writing goal—you will get to see your children more. Or perhaps becoming a successful author means you produce a beautiful chapbook of poetry that you can pass down to your grandkids, thereby creating a legacy of your life. The emotional component of that goal is that you create a legacy of your life; the value here might be "family historian." Maybe you strive to get your novels on the *New York Times* bestseller list because you want to be known in your genre as an outstanding writer. There's nothing wrong with that as a long-term goal. Attributes and traits associated with this goal and the corresponding Writer Self-Image might include "overcome a challenge" or "persistent." A writer who wants to pen articles that help animals and children would have attributes and values that define her in a role that makes a difference. An aspiring author who wants to finish a novel to prove to herself that she can do it would have values that reflect a disciplined, motivated person.

The emotional component of goals, the *why*, connects you to your positive Writer Self-Image because it personifies your attributes, traits, and values. The reasons why you want to accomplish your writing goals defines you as an author; it illuminates your motivations, creates feelings of enthusiasm, and generates behaviors that spur you on to the writing. When looking at the reasons behind *why* you write, you are getting to the core characteristics that define you as a writer and you are beginning to formulate your Writer Self-Image. Here, you are beginning to form the foundation of your thought patterns that will help you to bring the craft of writing into your daily life.

Activity: Define Your Writer Self-Image

In your journal, write down your writing goals. In another column, write down the emotional component, or why you want to achieve that goal. Beside that, give some thought to the values, attributes, and traits that spring from your *why*. The why represents the self-fulfilling prophecy you want to create. Last, write a one-sentence statement that defines your Writer Self-Image. Here are a few examples to get you started:

Writing Goal	Why I want to achieve this goal	Attributes, Traits, and Values of this why	Writer Self-Image statements
Finish my memoir	Knowing that my life will be remembered after I am gone; leave our family's history to my grandchildren	Family historian; document how I overcame challenges to give others encouragement and inspiration to do the same.	I am the family historian who will leave a legacy for my grandchildren that documents how I overcame challenges in order to give them inspiration and encouragement to do the same.
Write a book about important issue X	Help others; make a difference	Hard-working; give inspiration to others to work for change on this issue	I am a hard-working writer who will motivate and inspire others through my writing to work for change on issue X.
Make the <u>New York Times</u> bestseller List	A feeling of accomplishment, overcoming a challenge, achieving a big goal	Persistent, self-disciplined, motivated	I am a persistent and self-disciplined aspiring author who will write a bestselling novel and prove that I am an outstanding author in this genre.

Once you've created your chart, transfer your Writer Self-Image statement to a clean sheet of paper and hang it somewhere that you will see it every day. Whenever you feel your enthusiasm, motivation, and dedication to your long-term writing goals floundering, review your image statement. Doing so will reinforce to your subconscious mind the type of Writer Self-Image you are striving to create. It will generate thoughts, feelings, and behaviors consistent with the type of self-image you are striving to attain, and will set you up with a positive self-fulfilling prophecy.

On the accompanying CD, track two is designed to help you visualize this positive, successful Writer Self-Image. Please use it to help you complete this exercise.

Live Your Life Write

Your Writer Self-Image is a compilation of the attributes, traits, and values that define you as an author. It's a way of thinking, feeling, and behaving that inspires you to bring more writing into your daily life. Remember:

- The reasons *why* you want to attain your writing goals are an integral part of your Writer Self-Image.
- How you interpret events related to your writing depends upon a positive or negative Writer Self-Image.
- A positive Writer Self-Image creates a positive self-fulfilling prophecy.

Chapter 3

Your *Vision* of *Success* *Plus*

PART OF WHAT KEEPS MANY WRITERS WRITING EVERY DAY and working toward their long-term goals is the ability to see the big picture. Successful authors have an overall vision of where they want to go with their writing and the big goals they want to achieve. They begin their writing journey with the end in mind. The Burning Desire to Write, or that feeling that you can't not write, creates what I call a Vision of Success. This vision represents the writer's ideal self-image and self-fulfilling prophecy. It is her dream.

As an aspiring author, you already have the Burning Desire to Write, but you also need a Vision of Success that will give you direction and a target to aim for. It will help you to write or take some action toward your writing dream every day because you realize the importance of daily actions that establish the route for you to achieve long-term results.

Even better than a Vision of Success is a Vision of Success *Plus*—a vision with milestones or touchstones that aid you as you work your way toward your writing dreams.

Your Vision of Success *Plus*

Successful authors plan. Their daily actions have direction, method, and purpose. Your Vision of Success directs your daily writing habits and is linked to the reasons you listed in Chapter 2 about why you want to achieve your goals. It is the emotional dream you are chasing.

As with all successful authors, it may take years if not the rest of your life to fulfill your vision. Because of this, it's important to have small stepping stones or milestones along the way that mark your progress and give you encouragement to keep moving ahead. These milestones are your goals—the means to the end in terms of reaching your Vision of Success. They provide the stepping stones that aid you along the way as you strive to achieve your dream and they turn your Vision of Success into a Vision of Success *Plus*. Think of your Vision of Success *Plus* as a business plan for your writing; it looks at where you are, where you want to go, and how you're going to get there.

The Write Stuff

"I like five-year plans. They keep me focused on the big picture without being too big."

—Novelist Barbara O'Neal

Anna Hackett, author of *Hunter's Surrender* and other novels, wrote a business plan when she was a newly aspiring author. Her Vision of Success *Plus* is comprehensive. "It contains my goals, mission statement, an analysis of what I like about the writing of my favorite authors, what I think is unique about my stories, and promotion plans," she explains.

Notice how Hackett's plan is both short and long-term in scope. "My short-term goals cover the next year, my medium-term goals the next five years, and then I have a long-term goals section," she says.

Having a short- and long-term perspective in your Vision of Success *Plus* is a key element; Hackett helped herself out by making sure she had milestones to encourage her along the way—and you can too.

How to Create Milestones

Motivational speaker and author Brian Tracy says that people overestimate how much they can accomplish in one year but underestimate how much they can accomplish in five years or longer. This is one reason why people fail at their goals; they create too much expectation for a twelve-month period while overlooking the roominess that setting five-year or longer goals can provide.

Setting herself up to try and achieve the impossible was, at first, a trouble spot for Amber Leigh Williams, author of *Denied Origin*. "When I began writing full-time, I pushed myself very hard," she says. "I set goals that were impossible to reach, so there was always a sense of unfulfillment when I didn't reach them, despite the fact that I couldn't have humanly achieved them in many cases. Now I've learned to pace myself and reaching even small goals is much more rewarding than killing myself trying to reach those unattainable ones from years ago."

Setting realistic milestones for your vision sets you up for a greater likelihood of success. Cynthia Eden, author of *I'll Be Slaying You* and other novels, gives an example of a Vision of Success *Plus* that is both ambitious and practical at the same time. "When I first began writing, I started with simple goals. I wanted to final in writing contests. That was step one for me," she says. "When I started to get positive feedback, I moved to step two: submitting to publishers. I began my career with small publishers, and when I felt confident and ready, I decided to move to step three: obtaining an agent. Then I went to step four: submitting to New

York publishers. My current plan is to continue writing for New York and hopefully to branch out into additional genres and sub-genres in the years to come."

That is a great example of a Vision of Success *Plus*, one that moves steadily along toward long-term goals. You create what works for you. The various milestones that you can choose to include in your Vision of Success *Plus* include one-, three-, five-, ten-, and twenty-year goals. Let's look now at how to set those marks.

One-Year Mark

Goals that you want to achieve in twelve months should be highly realistic. Remember, most people overestimate what they can accomplish in a year. This is because a year seems like a long time at the beginning of the twelve months, but time passes swiftly, and you have a lot of other things to do besides work on your writing goals. So the key with one-year goal setting is to be realistic.

Also, it is a fact of life that whenever you set goals, unforeseen obstacles will arise that will throw you off track. When setting twelve-month goals, ask yourself what could happen over the next year that would prevent you from accomplishing the goal. Then ask yourself what you will do to work around it. Planning for obstacles, even when you do not know what they might be, helps you avoid losing all progress toward your vision whenever the obstacles show up. For instance, you or a family member might become ill, which could set you back a few weeks in your plans. Or, you might have to take an unexpected trip for business. Or you might change jobs and have a longer commute than you do now, so your writing time has to be adjusted. And so forth. Antic-ipate obstacles and build in flexibility to adapt to them.

I find it helpful to think of twelve-month writing goals in terms of *finishing* something: finish a novel, finish a book proposal, fin-ish reading five craft books, and so forth. "Finishing" goals feels doable, takes some of the pressure off as you move through the year, and brings a satisfying sense of closure when they are reached.

Your Vision of Success *Plus* is the culmination of the actions you need to take today to reach that vision. Ask yourself every day, "Am I doing something toward my writing dream?" Even if you only write 100 words per day, the small things you do now will accumulate over time.

Three-Year Mark

Three-year goals retain the sense of immediacy of one-year goals while allowing you to stretch and strive for bigger things than you can realistically accomplish in one year. They offer a friendly mid-point between one and five years where you can make adjustments if things get off track.

Award-winning novelist Nancy Martin, author *The Blackbird Sisters* series, uses the three-year mark as an instrument in her career planning. "Every three years I re-evaluate where I am and where I want to be," she says.

To create three-year milestones, review your one-year goals and imagine that you have achieved them. Consider what will happen after the year has passed; what is the next step? If you used a finishing goal as mentioned above, what will you do with your finished product? Look for an agent, start another book, attend a big conference, or pitch to your dream editor? For three-year milestones, think bigger than you did for your one-year mark, but again, set yourself up for success. Dream big, but plan realistically. Anticipate obstacles and brainstorm solutions for meeting your goals around those obstacles.

Five-Year Mark

Five-year milestones are where you want to start getting traction toward your Vision of Success, and "results" goals are ideal for your five-year milestones. Five-year results goals are exactly what the name implies: goals that will start producing visible results within five years. For example, Cynthia Eden used the five-year mark for her results goal of getting published. "At the start of my plan, I gave myself five years to publish," she says. "I didn't expect overnight success. I knew this was a career that would take time. At the end of five years, I planned to re-evaluate and see which goals I had accomplished."

Five-year results goals provide evidence that you are on the right track for achieving your Vision of Success *Plus* because you begin seeing the fruits of your labor. In addition to getting published, other examples of five-year results goals might be signing with an agent, finishing a trilogy, or self-publishing your poetry chapbook.

Ten-Year Mark

Ten years is a long time. You can do a lot of writing and can achieve a lot of things in ten years. For your ten-year milestones, visualize elements of your Vision of Success manifesting. Ten-year milestones include "accomplishment" goals or the things you want to have achieved. Examples might be finishing a second trilogy, winning a writing award, becoming a recognized expert on a certain topic, making a bestseller list, and so forth.

Twenty-Year Milestones

Your twenty-year milestones are your Vision of Success achieved. What do you want to have accomplished in two decades of writing? This is not the time to be critical or small-thinking; it's a time to dream and dream big. The Vision of Success is your ideal writing life and your ideal Writer Self-Image. Examples of milestones here might include making multiple bestseller lists, making a living as an author, having a certain number of books published, and so on.

The Write Stuff

"'What am I doing today that will allow me to reach X goal in one year?' The shorter the time frame, the more I have to be working toward it right now."

—Author Mary Buckham

Backward Chaining

Another way to create milestones is to use a process known in psychology as backward chaining. Backward chaining involves starting at the end of a task and figuring out in reverse the steps needed to get there. Essentially, you work backwards. Start at your end goal, your twenty-year goal, and move back to the ten-year mark, then the five-year mark, then the three-year mark, then the one-year mark.

For example, let's say that in twenty years you want to be writing science fiction novels for a living. To use the backward chaining process, work backwards to identify steps and mile-stones that you will need to reach along the way. Ask yourself what major accomplishment or milestone you would have achieved right before beginning to write novels for a living. It might be something along the lines of getting a certain number of books published for a certain amount of money; maybe you want to have at least ten novels in circulation and be receiving a certain amount in royalties each year. The step behind that at five years might be acquiring literary representation. An agent has to have a manuscript to sell, so your three-year milestone might be to have a polished, publication-ready manuscript.

Now that you are at the three-year milestone, the steps become a bit more meaty. You will begin to see the actual actions you need to take now in order to reach your Vision of Success. Continuing to work backwards, consider what you need to do in order to have a novel to polish. To finish a novel you have to write the novel and you might want to take some craft classes or attend workshops before you finish that up. So your milestone at year three might be to have taken a certain number of classes and have attended a certain number of conferences. What is the step behind that for your one-year milestone? It's probably to sit down and write on a consistent basis in order to have a draft of the novel that you can then polish.

Using backward chaining helps you work your way down to the ground floor of your Vision of Success and helps you identify achievable milestones along the way.

Striking a Balance Between Dreams and Reality

As you work on your Vision of Success *Plus*, keep in mind that what you are trying to achieve is a balance between your dreams and reality. You do not want to throw cold water on your dreams, but you also want to ensure that you set yourself up for success. Striking a balance between dreams and reality is a challenge for all writers at all stages of their careers. "It's a back and forth thing between jumping imaginatively into the future and back to the here and now and today's word count," says Harley Jane Kozak, the award-winning author of *Dating Dead Men* and other novels. "If I stay too much in the future, I freak out at the great gulf between the novel I envision and the meager chapters I have on paper."

Having a Vision of Success *Plus* is a good way to help you navigate the empty space between your dreams and your current reality. The beauty and irony of your vision is that it actually helps dictate your daily behaviors because it's what you do now, and day after day, that will determine whether or not you ever reach those one-, three-, five-, ten-, and twenty-year milestones that make up your Vision of Success.

For example, a goal of my twenty-year Vision of Success is to have written (and hopefully published) a certain number of books. Knowing that gives me direction now, twenty years ahead of time, on how to proceed. If I want to get my goal number of manuscripts written in twenty years, I have to write every day. Books don't write themselves, and if I want to meet that twenty-year goal, I had better start writing now. That's the real beauty of a Vision of a Success; you can use it to guide your present behaviors in order to achieve long-term, substantial results. Long-range planning, ironically, drives you to bring more writing into your daily life.

Novelist Lori Foster figured out early on that long-term goals can be lofty, but the short-term steps to attain them must be doable and small. "My goals have all been short-term and very realistic," she explains. "I know certain things are entirely out of my control, so I set goals for the things that I know I can achieve. For instance, my goal was never to sell. My goal was to write a book good enough to sell, and then to cross my fingers for the rest. My goals will be to write a chapter, to nail down a conflict, et cetera."

But after Foster got published, she included milestones in her Vision of Success that would not have been conceivable before she was published. "My goals also included, after I'd sold, achieving certain things within the contract. Getting cover approval was a huge goal of mine," she says.

As Foster's example illustrates, creating a Vision of Success *Plus* is a fluid process that helps you focus on both the long-term prize and the short-term actions you can take now to make that Vision a reality.

Benefits of a Vision of Success *Plus*

There are a number of benefits to having a Vision of Success *Plus* laid out for your writing future. Let's look at the ways this type of map can help not only your writing career but also support the daily writing habits that will lead you to long-term success and help you bring the craft of writing into your daily life.

Gives You a Stable Target

You can't hit a moving target. A Vision of Success *Plus* gives you a stable goal to aim for even if some of your smaller milestone goals change. This comes in handy when circumstances happen that are beyond your control. For instance, let's say your goal is to publish fiction titles but your nonfiction work unexpectedly takes off and you find yourself working more in that category for a while. Despite this detour, your core vision remains constant, but the way you get there can change. Keeping your end goal of writing and publishing fiction in mind, your Vision of Success stabilizes you as you navigate the detours and move ahead in your journey.

Focuses Your Daily Efforts

The milestones that comprise your Vision of Success *Plus* dictate your daily writing actions. Remember, it's what you do now, today, that will determine whether or not you achieve your Vision of Success. The milestones indicate the tiny actions you need to take right now that will inch you closer to your dream. If your one-year milestone is to finish your novel, you can't spend every weekend in front of the television watching ESPN. You have to get to your desk and write every single day. Daily writing is the foundation of success for your writing dreams.

This is a way that Mary Buckham, author of *Break Into Fiction: 11 Steps to Building a Story That Sells* and other books, uses her Vision of Success *Plus*. Notice, too, how she controls her thoughts in order to direct her behaviors toward her writing goals. "I'm always looking one, three, and five years out at a minimum," she says. "That gives me a sense of perspective and helps create my daily questions such as, 'What am I doing today that will allow me to reach X goal in one year?' The shorter the time frame, the more I have to be working toward it right now, which creates clear, immediate focus versus vague, wouldn't-it-be nice dreams."

Just as Buckham's comment demonstrates, the milestones you set for yourself influence your thought-feeling-behavior cycle. Your day-to-day thoughts and feelings will direct your behaviors toward the small steps that create momentum for achieving your dream. When you identify milestones for your Vision of Success, you begin to feel enthusiastic, motivated, and dedicated. Your thoughts shift to reflect these feelings and in turn impact your behavior. Your thoughts, feelings, and behaviors move in a positive, goal-oriented direction. You begin programming your subconscious mind to help you think, feel, and act in ways that will bring about the milestones and ultimately achieve your Vision of Success.

Empowers You

A Vision of Success *Plus* empowers you to take actions that move you closer to your dream, and it helps you focus on the elements of your dream that you can control. In publishing, as in every business, unforeseen pitfalls arise as you move forward. A Vision of Success *Plus* keeps you on track and working on the pieces that are actually under your command. In the example I gave earlier about my twenty-year milestone, my vision is to *write* a certain number books in twenty years, not *publish* them. Of course I hope they will get published, but that is not something that I have ultimate control over, so it's not my goal. While there are efforts that I can make that will greatly enhance the chances that I will actually publish the books I write, the only thing I really have control over is whether or not I sit down and actually write the books. That is what dictates my daily action. If the books are not written, there is a 100 percent chance they won't get published. So my job between now and twenty years is simply to write the books.

Activity: Write Your Vision of Success Plus

It's time for you to map out a dream for your writing future. In your notebook, designate a separate section for your Vision of Success *Plus*. Write down your ultimate goal, your Vision of Success, and add the corresponding one-, three-, five-, ten-, and twenty-year milestones. If you are having difficulty coming up with milestones for the further reaching years, please make use of Track 4 on the accompanying CD.

CD Instructions

The purpose of the CD session is to help you program your subconscious to begin building your Vision of Success *Plus* with corresponding milestones.

For this session, you will use a mild state of relaxation, so find a place where you will not be disturbed and eliminate noise sources, distractions, and turn the lights to a comfortable level. You will need your digital recorder easily accessible because, as soon as the relaxation process has been completed, you will be instructed to start recording the thoughts that will come to mind as you build your Vision of Success *Plus*.

Live Your Life Write

Your Vision of Success *Plus* is a blueprint for your long-term writing success and a way to create daily actions that will bring more writing to your life. Remember:

- Most people overestimate what they can accomplish in one year but underestimate what they can accomplish in three, five, ten, and twenty years.
- The goal of a Vision of Success *Plus* is to allow you to dream big while setting concrete milestones for how you will achieve your long-term writing success.
- The backward-chaining process allows you start with a large goal and work backwards in order to more accurately pinpoint the smaller steps required to achieve the goal.
- Benefits of having a Vision of Success *Plus* include focusing your behaviors on a daily basis that lead to success and a positive self-fulfilling prophecy, helping you navigate unforeseen obstacles over the years, and giving you a sense of empowerment over your writing career.

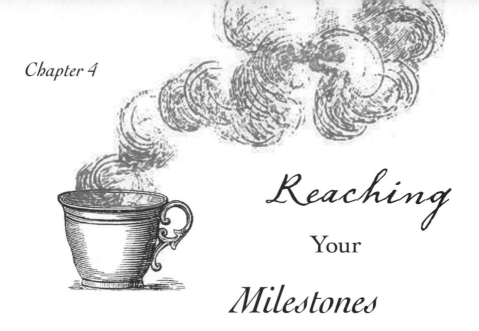

Chapter 4

Reaching
Your
Milestones

IN THE LAST CHAPTER, YOU CREATED A VISION OF SUCCESS *Plus* that places you and your writing dream one, three, five, ten, and twenty years into the future. The corresponding milestones give you guideposts as you navigate your way toward reaching your dream. The milestones help you take action every day toward achieving your Vision of Success.

But let's take this idea one step further and discuss how you can capitalize on your thought-feeling-behavior cycle to help reach your milestones and become the writer you are striving to be.

Keep Your Thoughts on Your Milestones

A simple yet effective way to go about achieving your milestones is to simply think about them all the time. Your thoughts guide your behaviors, which in turn guide the way you spend your day, every day. In turn, your individual days build your future, little by little. For the aspiring writer, it's important to have thoughts that support your writing milestones, your positive Writer Self-Image, and your positive self-fulfilling prophecy.

The way to keep your thoughts trained in a positive direction is to keep your eye on your Vision of Success while you work day to day to achieve it. Remember, daily actions are important. This is a strategy of most successful authors. "I spend a lot of time daydreaming about the big picture," says award-winning novelist Harley Jane Kozak, "and then figuring out how that translates to small steps."

To do this, read your Vision of Success *Plus* every day. Write your milestones in the form of goals. Keep your list of replacement thoughts that you created in Chapter 1 handy. Feel the good feelings associated with them. If you catch yourself having a negative thought, immediately read your replacement thought. This will keep your mind trained on your Vision of Success *Plus* and your individual milestones.

Get Energy from Your Positive Thoughts

Thoughts have a cumulative effect on the subconscious mind; over time and with enough repetition, they program the subconscious mind to bring about the outcomes of the accumulated thoughts. This is why any negative statement—no matter how small—will eventually bring about the negative conditions of those thoughts if the thought is frequently repeated. For instance, the negative statement "I don't know how to write a book" will leave you demoralized, discouraged, and utterly unmotivated to make an attempt at writing. How can anyone with that type of thought running through their head, even as background noise, have any hope of feeling like writing? It's impossible. It drains your energy and replaces it with a hopeless state of mind that leads to stagnation and more frustration.

On the other hand, positive thoughts charge you up—they encourage and inspire you to take the actions that help you reach your milestones. Changing the above statement to, "I will write this book one page at a time" boosts you up, gives you a burst of energy, and compels you to take action. Say it out loud and see if it doesn't do that for you. The behavior that follows a positive thought or feeling like that is one that ushers you forward toward reaching your milestones. When you think about it that way, writing a book one page at a time sounds exciting. It sounds doable; it motivates, inspires, and enthuses you to get to your desk and write. Positive thoughts and feelings drive you to take action that will bring about your Vision of Success *Plus*.

The Write Stuff

"I set goals for the things that I know I can achieve."

—Novelist Lori Foster

Take Action

Taking action—any action—is usually better than doing nothing when it comes to reaching the milestones in your vision. Well-chosen behaviors that improve your Writer Self-Image will elicit thoughts and feelings that build you up and enhance your chances for success.

The trouble many people have is *thinking* about being a writer without *acting* like a writer. Make a commitment to take action toward your dream, no matter where you are on the career ladder. A good place to start is to simply write every day. You can also read books similar to the ones you want to write. Attend workshops. Join a writer's critique group and share your work with peers who will be helpful and supportive but also push you to improve your skills.

Action is the strongest and most effective way to program your subconscious mind to bring about your Vision of Success *Plus*— action sets up the thoughts and feelings *after the fact* that will help you meet your long-term writing goals. Taking action toward your writing milestones generates enthusiasm, motivation, and dedication to keep working toward your writing dreams.

Don't Feel Like Writing? Do It Anyway

You may be familiar with the saying, usually attributed to Virginia Woolf, that she didn't like writing but she liked having written. That is a good example of how just taking the action of writing generates dedication and motivation after the writer has made the decision to sit down at the desk—no matter how she is feeling. Madeleine L'Engle said, "Inspiration comes during work, not before it." This is a good example of the power of action. Again, action (behavior) creates the thoughts and feelings that stimulate enthusiasm, motivation, and dedication.

Put yourself in this situation for a moment. Imagine not feeling like writing but going ahead and fulfilling your writing schedule anyway. How does it make you feel to imagine yourself meeting your word or page count quota for the day? It probably makes you feel good. You're likely to have a deep-seated sense of fulfillment and find yourself eager to return to the desk the next day. You have fulfilled your Burning Desire to Write.

Daily Direction

Use writing something fun as a reward for writing something difficult. For instance, to get through a difficult point in your story, visualize an upcoming scene that you are excited to write. Then, tell yourself that you can write the fun scene as soon as you finish the difficult one.

It's easy to think about writing the next day when you have touched that deep inner well and have finished what you said you would do today. But when you avoid writing and resist getting to the desk for days on end it gets harder and harder to get there. Obstacles to writing get bigger the more you avoid facing them. This is because, as I mentioned before, negative thoughts build on each other (as do positive thoughts) and, with enough repetition, they program your subconscious mind to create the reality of the thought. If you constantly avoid writing, you will likely create within yourself a fear of the blank page or fear of failure, and will likely feel intimidated by the hugeness of the project you are facing. The thoughts that spin off from those feelings are probably along the lines of those listed earlier: "I can't do this" or "I don't know how to write a book" or "This will take too long to finish."

Taking action to overcome those thoughts and feelings is an easy and quick way to cut through the fog created by that negativity and start moving forward again. So just sit down to write whether you feel like it or not.

Write with Your Eyes Closed

Bestselling author CJ Lyons recommends that writers, when they don't feel like writing, sit down anyway and start typing with their eyes closed, just to get the feeling of their fingers moving over the keyboard, which can jump-start the creative mind. This technique capitalizes on the component of feelings. When you sit down and run your fingers over the keyboard, you feel like you are writing and therefore become inspired to write. You begin having thoughts about your work-in-progress and the behavior of writing follows. I have used this technique myself, and it works— it's a great way to ease into the day's writing.

"I spend a lot of time daydreaming about the big picture and then figuring out how that translates to small steps."

—Novelist Harley Jane Kozak

Pretend

Another way to use the component of feelings is to pretend that you already feel the way you want to feel. If you want to feel inspired, pretend that you are inspired. If you want to feel enthused about your work-in-progress, pretend to feel enthusiastic. Make statements like, "This is the best novel I've ever written." Mean it. Notice how you feel. Pretend that you are as excited and happy with your work-in-progress, no matter what shape it's in, as you will be the day it lands in bookstores.

Have Flexibility

Your Vision of Success *Plus* will remain constant as you move ahead with implementing your writing plans. However, it's important for you to remain flexible when it comes to the specifics of your milestones.

Novelist Mary Buckham gives an example of how her Vision of Success *Plus* stayed the same over time even when her individual milestones changed. "The way I intend to reach my goals can be in flux, but the goals themselves do not change that much," she says. "For example, writing a book to be published by one of the New York publishing houses is an end goal, but which publishing house can change, and what genre I'm writing can change. But not the end goal. Life changes, but keeping the eye on the big prizes helps dictate flexibility and focus day to day."

In the same way, you can adapt your milestones as you move along.

Use Visualization

Visualizing capitalizes on the component of thought in the thought-feeling-behavior cycle. Using directed and concentrated thought through the technique of visualization programs your subconscious mind to bring about the outcome you are thinking about.

There are a myriad of ways to use visualization to reach your milestones. If you want to increase the number of days you write every week, picture a calendar with the days of the week and then imagine yourself writing each of those days. Visualize the finished manuscript you are working on it. Picture yourself mailing it off and receiving an acceptance letter from an agent. Visualize your books in the bookstore and in a special place in your own home.

I use visualization frequently to meet my daily writing schedule. Before I go to bed, I picture myself getting up before dawn the next morning and going to my desk to write. Visualizing the next scene to be written is a tool that inspires novelist Amber Leigh Williams to achieve her daily milestones. "To get myself motivated, I visualize a scene or sequence later in the plot that I'm looking forward to writing and tell myself that the more I write today, the closer I am to getting to the fun stuff," she says. "That's the true reward—writing those scenes that get the adrenaline pumping."

Set Daily Tasks

Successful writers plan their days around their writing. Even if you can only write for thirty minutes, plan your day around those thirty minutes. Remember that action is the most effective programmer of your subconscious mind because it influences your thoughts and feelings in powerful ways.

Novelist Cynthia Eden describes how daily tasks move her along toward her long-term writing goals. "Every day, I determine to write a set number of pages, usually ten pages a day," she says. "I don't go to bed at night unless I've met those writing goals. By completing my writing goals, I can actually see my progress as the page count increases and that serves to motivate me even more."

Daily Direction

To motivate yourself to write every day, give yourself a quarter every time you complete your word or page count goal. When you have finished your work-in-progress, use the accumulated change to treat yourself.

Pick Your Most Powerful Element and Capitalize on It

Remember that the thought-feeling-behavior cycle is circular; each component has the ability to impact and change the other two. Most people have one element that is more influential than the other two, and that is the element you should hone in on and try to impact the most. Perhaps you are the kind of person who has feelings and thoughts impacted by actual behavior or action-taking. If so, it's important for you to follow through on any behavioral milestones that you set for yourself in your Vision of Success *Plus*. If you are more inspired by thoughts, hone in on positive thoughts that help you achieve your milestones. If feelings are your most powerful element, generate feelings of enthusiasm, dedication, and motivation to your writing goals by visualizing your dreams coming true.

Activity: Reach Your Milestones Through Thoughts, Feelings, and Behaviors

Review the list of milestones you created in the last chapter. In your notebook, make a list of the thoughts, feelings, and behaviors that you can cultivate to reach each of those milestones. Focus on the element of the thought-feeling-behavior cycle that is the strongest for you. If you need to improve upon your writing frequency and thoughts are your key element, make a list of thoughts you can tell yourself to reach this milestone. If feelings are your most influential component, list the feelings you need to have in order to reach your milestones. Do this for each of your one-, three-, and five-year milestones at a minimum.

Live Your Life Write

Fulfillment of your Vision of Success *Plus* depends on your daily actions, and your actions are based on your thoughts and feelings. To ensure that your writing future is a success, remember:

- Thoughts are cumulative in nature and will eventually program your subconscious to bring about your reality.
- Catch your negative thoughts so that you can redirect them into more positive energies. A good way to notice negative thoughts about your writing is to observe your feelings about writing.
- Not feeling like writing is the bane of many aspiring writers and has the tendency to get worse the more writing is avoided. Taking action to write even when you do not feel like it is a good way to change your thoughts and feelings about your writing and your abilities as a writer.

Chapter 5

The *"I"* in *Image* Is You

As we discussed in Chapter 2, your Writer Self-Image is a collection of attributes, traits, and values that make up who you are as a writer. This self-image manifests itself in how you think, feel, and behave toward your writing. A critical part of maintaining a positive Writer Self-Image is to keep your thought-feeling-thought cycle positive and goal directed. One way to do this is by taking responsibility for your own success as a writer. Here, we will discuss how taking responsibility for your writing and your desired writing outcomes enhances your chances of success and strengthens your Writer Self-Image.

Taking Charge of Your Thoughts

You have complete responsibility for maintaining your Writer Self-Image at all times. Because of that, it's important to work toward staying positive and goal-oriented under all circumstances. Maintaining a positive Writer Self-Image means that you let discouragement and rejection bounce right off of you.

That's sometimes easier said than done. When something goes wrong with your plans—when an essay you thought was a sure thing is rejected, when your top agent declines to represent you, when a pitch at a conference tanks—it's easy to become discouraged and to internalize that rejection. You may get down on yourself and feel like giving up. This damages your Writer Self-Image because when you do this, you give control of that image to an external person or situation. Maintaining a solid Writer Self-Image means taking full responsibility for your image at all times and keeping it intact. When you find yourself thinking and feeling damaging statements, it's important to stop, catch what you are doing, and reverse your thought-feeling-thought cycle in order to preserve a solid, positive, goal-directed Writer Self-Image.

The Write Stuff

"Every day I try to write a minimum of five pages. Those pages might be terrible. But at least they're something I can work with later."

—Award-winning author Nancy Martin

Thought on Thought

Let me give you an example from my own writing life. Many years ago, I pitched a novel idea to an agent at a conference. This novel was one that I felt particularly good about since I had worked on it for about a year. I had completed several writing classes and learned new skills that I applied to the book. Critique partners had been enthusiastic about the novel and given me good feedback. But within two minutes of the actual pitch, I could tell the agent wasn't interested. I pressed on, held on to my positive attitude, but to no avail. The pitch session ended, I thanked her for her time, and left the room.

Because I had felt so great about the book before going into the pitch session, this agent's rejection left me feeling discouraged. I started to think that my critique partners had been wrong. That got me thinking that maybe the book idea wasn't that great after all. My mood plunged, and my thoughts and Writer Self-Image continued downward on a slippery slope.

This went on for about fifteen minutes before I caught myself. I realized that I had allowed something outside of myself—an agent's feedback—to influence my internal thought-feeling-thought cycle, which in turn was trouncing my Writer Self-Image. To reverse it, I had to do something fast.

"I" Statements

One way to reverse a negatively spiraling thought-feeling-thought cycle is to use "I" statements. The use of "I" statements in psychology is a reliable method of helping people take responsibility for their own lives and helping them understand the concept of changing their feelings in goal directed ways. When a person takes responsibility for his own life through the use of "I" statements, the results are a positive change in his behavior, an increased feeling of control over his life, and improved environmental circumstances that are more conducive to success.

Here is how I used it in the above example. I stopped myself from thinking any further negative thoughts by shouting "Stop!" in my head. This technique is called thought-blocking. It's useful whenever you find yourself in a spiraling thought-on-thought situation that you want to take control of immediately. You can also visualize a giant stop sign flinging up in your mind, you can verbally say the word stop, you can clap your hands, ring a bell, snap a rubber band on your wrist, or use any other technique that gets your conscious mind's focus back under your control.

The Write Stuff

"I have kept in mind that the only
person who can stop me is me.
No one can publish me if I don't keep trying!"

—Novelist Debra Webb

Once I had stopped the cycle of negative thoughts, I could reverse them. I began to think more clearly. I realized that the reality of this particular situation was that minutes before I had to go in to do my pitch, I received an upsetting phone call from home. I was too rattled to do the pitch, but I did not feel that I could ask the conference staff to change my pitch time because they had already changed it once to accommodate my workshop presentation.

All this gave me grist for the mill for changing my thoughts and feelings about the unsuccessful pitch session. I did this by using "I" statements; I took responsibility not only for the pitch, but for my manuscript. Here are the "I" statements that I made:

- "I did not present the novel in a way that interested that particular agent."
- "I will find an agent who loves this book."
- "I have written a book that will be successful."
- "I was off my game this morning; I will be successful next time."

Notice that the statements all reflect my personal responsibility in the situation. None of them make the agent or any source or situation outside myself responsible for giving a good pitch, selling the book, or creating my overall success as a writer. I accept responsibility for all of it. Even though I did receive an upsetting call before I went in, I still had choice in the matter. I could have canceled the pitch session since I was too rattled to give it well. Or I could go in, do it to the best of my ability, and let the chips fall where they may. I chose the latter, and the chips didn't fall where I would have preferred them to fall. But still, it was my choice, my responsibility, to go into that pitch session.

Clearly there are situations and circumstances that you cannot control; an agent or editor's ultimate like or dislike of your book, the size of that agent's client load or if he is taking new authors, whether or not she woke up with a headache that day or spilled her coffee or burned her hand on the iron. The point is, you cannot control everything, but you can take responsibility for the outcome of *your* actions. When you internalize responsibility for your own success through the use of "I" statements, you take back control of your own career, you feel more powerful, and you stop the negative thought-feeling-thought cycle that is a byproduct of feeling powerless and out of control.

Daily Direction

Take ownership for your daily writing actions by accepting full responsibility for the days you do not write, even if something happens that is beyond your control. Doing this strengthens your resolve to meet your writing goal the next day.

You can also use "I" statements to take responsibility for your daily actions toward writing. State this out loud: "I am responsible for writing every day." If one day you do not write, even if it was because of circumstances beyond your control, take responsibility. Declare that you chose not to write that day. Then get back to your schedule the next day. Take full responsibility for meeting your daily writing goals, no matter what happens.

Taking responsibility through the use of "I" statements feels good. It empowers you. Create your own "I" statements to see how it works.

Activity: Create Your "I" Statements

In this activity, you will begin to change your thought-feeling-thought cycle in positive, goal directed ways. Take a few of the problem thoughts from your list in Chapter 1 and transfer them to a new page in your journal. Write down the corresponding feeling as well.

Next, take a few minutes to identify a thought that sprang from the original negative thought; it's likely that this second thought only worsened your feeling. Write that down. Last, create an "I" statement that shifts the focus and responsibility for your success back to you and to things you can control.

The table that follows illustrates a few examples that will help to get you started:

Thought #1	Feeling	Thought #2	"I" statements (positive, goal directed)
I have submitted my manuscript to twenty agents and none of them have taken it. Something is wrong with my writing.	Discouraged	I must not be a very good writer or have very good ideas since no one has accepted me as a client.	I will succeed as a writer. I have an abundance of perseverance. I will succeed if I keep working my plan.
I never have time to write.	Hopeless	I am never going to get that novel finished.	I know there is time in my day to write and I will find it. If I look for the time, it will be there. I will make writing a priority in my day.
I just don't feel like writing right now.	Disappointed	My muse has taken a permanent vacation.	I am a successful writer and successful writers do not wait for their muse to show up. If I start writing, inspiration will arrive.

Live Your Life Write

Using "I" statements is a reliable method of influencing your thoughts and feelings in ways that positively affect your behaviors in goal-directed ways. Learning to take responsibility for the events in your writing life that you can control leads to an enhancement of your Writer Self-Image in powerful ways. It creates more confidence in your abilities and raises your self-esteem. All of this impacts your thought-feeling-behavior cycle in ways that lead you to act in ways that are more likely to manifest success. Remember:

- Thoughts build on other thoughts and generate feelings that affect your behavior.
- Focus on and implement behaviors that you have control over to enhance your Writer Self-Image.
- Identify the thoughts that are creating negative feelings about your Writer Self-Image and create "I" statements to combat them.

part ii

Developing A Writer's Mind-Set

In this part, we will talk about ways that you can begin to develop a writer's mind-set. Creating a writer's mind-set is important to your success because it establishes a specific perspective under which you operate on a day-to-day basis. Writing becomes a priority. You give it time and attention each and every day. A writer's mind-set makes forming the daily writing habit easier because your subconscious locks in on the image of you as a writer and helps you design your time so that you can meet your writing goals. Ensuring that writing becomes a much bigger part of your daily life is part of a successful writer's mind-set. There are other strategies for developing a writer's mind-set, too, such as overcoming self-doubt, using a role-model to improve your writing habits, and Image Incorporation to achieve positive changes in your writing life that we'll discuss here.

Chapter 6

Overcoming Self-Doubt

Self-doubt is the elephant in the room for most writers. It's a problem that no one likes to talk about it because it's an uncomfortable issue. Self-doubt is the opposite of a positive Writer Self-Image; it's a small but nagging thought that undermines your efforts toward your writing goals. Self-doubt keeps you from writing every day because it weakens your belief in yourself as a writer.

If self-doubt is interfering with your efforts to find success as a writer, however you define that success, you need to take a look at how it is affecting you and change your thought-feeling-behavior cycle to overcome it. Self-doubt can be your downfall unless you take steps to combat it.

Let's take a look at the issue of self-doubt and how you can manage it in your own writing life.

Self-Sabotaging

There is a theory in psychology called self-sabotaging. This theory asserts that the way people perform on any given task is based partially on their expectations of how they will perform. If they expect to fail, they will do something that handicaps them in some way and causes them to exert less effort on the task, making failure more likely. This fulfills a negative self-fulfilling prophecy.

This theory also asserts that people will take measures to protect their self-image when they strongly desire to achieve success in a certain endeavor but doubt their ability to do so. These people often create an obstacle to performing well in any given situation that would enhance chances of success on the task at hand.

The Write Stuff

"Doubt can be useful if you use it as a motive to keep striving to do even better."

—Novelist Debra Webb

Let's apply this theory to writing. If you desire success as a writer, and it's safe to assume you do since you are reading this book, but you genuinely doubt your abilities to achieve that success, it is highly probable that you will do something to sabotage your own efforts. You might do this in a number of the following ways:

- You avoid writing every day.
- You get to your desk but freeze up when you try to get words on the page.
- You do not push yourself to improve your writing skills as hard as you could.
- You write stories but never send them out.
- You avoid putting yourself in situations that could challenge you to grow as a writer, such as critique groups, conferences, and contests.
- You allow negative thoughts and feelings to impact your confidence.
- You miss deadlines.

As you can see, self-sabotaging manifests itself in different ways for different writers. For aspiring authors, the biggest self-sabotaging obstacle I see is avoiding writing, so let's turn our attention to that for a minute.

Avoidance Is a Self-Sabotaging Gesture

In many writing classes, people often cite avoidance as the biggest reason for failing to sit down and write the stories that are clanging around in their heads. Avoidance is the self-sabotaging measure of choice for many aspiring and published authors alike. Self-sabotaging avoidance comes in many disguises. You could avoid making a writing schedule, or you could avoid sitting down to write when the time comes. You could avoid improving your skills. You could avoid the tedious tasks that go along with becoming a writer, like rewriting first drafts, researching agents who accept your genre, or tracking your progress on completing your work-in-progress. All of these are avoidance measures that handicap you on your path to achieving success as a writer.

Related to Fear

Some of this avoidance is related to fear, both fear of failure and fear of success. The reason people fear success is because it represents change, and it is human nature to resist change of any kind, even when it's positive. But overcoming your self-sabotaging measures means challenging yourself to grow as a writer, stretch out of your comfort zone, and do things that feel scary and unnatural.

Ironically, even years of achievement may not alleviate the fear of success. All writers are striving to reach the top of their personal mountain. The key with self-sabotaging behaviors is to not let them interfere with the behaviors that are necessary to reach your long-term goals.

How to Overcome Self-Doubt

Self-doubt is that little voice inside your head that says, "I can't." Everyone, aspiring and published authors alike, hears this voice. "Doubt can be a constant companion for a writer," says novelist Cynthia Eden. "Is the story good enough? Are the characters believable? Will readers like the path I've taken for this story?"

Doubt is what causes you to self-sabotage. The trick is to change the "I can't" into "I can." Let's look at ways that successful authors manage self-doubt in their careers, and how you can incorporate these measures into your own daily writing routine.

Daily Direction

When self-doubt interferes with your efforts to write every day, write about your self-doubt. Getting your thoughts on to paper will help you sort through your feelings. Define your self-doubt as clearly as you can, then write about why it is not going to stop you from writing.

Revise and Rewrite

People often avoid writing day after day because they doubt that what they do write is any good. For many years, I had a problem with not wanting to reread my own material. I cringed at the idea of reading what I had written the day before because I was convinced it was terrible. Clearly, this is not a healthy response to your own work. You must be able to look at what you have written and see the good as well as the sections that need improving.

I overcame this tendency by learning to force myself to reread my earlier material at the beginning of each new writing session.

Eventually I learned that not *all* of it was awful. If this is a trouble spot for you, begin your writing day by pulling out yesterday's work and reading and editing it. Nine times out of ten, the material is not as bad as you think it's going to be. And easing into the day's writing through the side door of revising and rewriting is often enough to stimulate your creative flow and get the juices going.

For some writers, like award-winning author Nancy Martin, revising and rewriting is a way to challenge herself to work harder and get better and better. "I have plenty of self-doubt," she says. "I doubt myself every day. What helps me overcome those concerns is revising. The more I tinker with my words, improve my prose, make my storytelling clearer, the better the results. Nora Roberts once called it Author Paranoia. She said feeling inadequate has made her work harder and harder. I stand with Nora on this subject. The only thing you can do to be a better writer is to work at becoming a better writer."

Revising and rewriting is the way you become a better writer, and it's the way you learn to love your own work.

Just Start Writing

One of the easiest ways to overcome self-doubt is to just sit down and start getting words on the page. Simply move your fingers until words start flowing. Type anything. Type the alphabet. Type about what you do for a living. Take out a book and start typing any random page. Turn your inner critic off and allow your fingers to flow across the keyboard. Doing this jump starts your brain and gets your mind into alpha state, which has been shown to be conducive and necessary for creativity.

This technique has worked for me because I often have trouble with avoiding writing. As soon as I get a book contract, it seems like the last thing I want to do is sit down and actually write. Fear that I will not be able to write the book takes over, and I freeze up, and rather than trying to sit down and bang something out, I will usually fall into a pattern of sleeping too much, reading too much, and watching too much television. Not exactly the way to get a book written or to meet long-term writing goals, is it?

After a lot of teeth gnashing, I usually convince myself to just sit down and start typing. Most of it ends up being unusable material, but after a few minutes my mind slips into the alpha state and I can get back into my own material and get some writing done.

Consult Your Replacement Thoughts and Feelings

When you find yourself avoiding your writing, it's critical that you pay attention to your thoughts and feelings at that time. Define your feelings of self-doubt as clearly as you can; are you afraid of failure? Are you afraid of success? What might be causing these feelings and what are the thoughts behind the feelings? Have you tried at writing in the past, failed, and are now reticent to give it another try? Are your writing skills rusty from lack of use?

If you are avoiding writing due to these types of negative thoughts, sit down and write out positive replacement thoughts. State them out loud. Allow yourself to feel the sense of accomplishment you will enjoy when you have gotten your writing done for the day. Review your Vision of Success *Plus* and the actions you need to take to reach your milestones. Practice changing your thoughts and feelings in order to alter your behavior in a positive, goal-directed way.

Enter Contests

A good way to bolster your self-confidence and overcome self-doubt is to enter writing contests. Entering contests is sort of like practicing to submit your work to editors and agents. It gives you a way to get your work out there, but without the threat of actual rejection. It gives you practice in polishing a piece of work for another person to read. Even if you do not win, simply putting your work forward boosts your self-confidence because you believe in yourself and your work enough to send it out. Some contests also have a mechanism for getting feedback from the agents, editors, or published authors who are the judges.

Entering contests was one way that author Leslie Tentler kept her self-confidence levels high as she was working to learn the craft of writing. Tentler eventually finaled in a contest that resulted in her landing a contract for her first novel, *Midnight Caller*. "As a writer, you hear so much negative criticism, from others as well as from inside your own head," she says. "Having my work noticed in those contests was a boost that I tried to keep with me, to help weather those many, many times of self-doubt."

Most writing organizations hold contests as a way to raise money and increase membership. Look for groups in your genre and inquire about their annual contests. Many writing craft magazines also hold contests or make announcements about contests in various issues.

Entering contests also gives you a deadline to work toward; you are more likely to focus on your daily writing if you have the short-term goal of meeting that deadline in front of you.

The Write Stuff

"The only thing you can do to be a better writer is to work at becoming a better writer."

—Author Nancy Martin

How Rejection Helps You Overcome Self-Doubt

Some people never send out their work because they fear rejection. Others, upon receiving their first rejection letter, feel utterly discouraged. Some give up after a while; others wallpaper their bedrooms with rejection letters (which only serves to impress the idea of failure on to the subconscious mind, which is why I recommend that you do not do this).

It may seem counterintuitive, but the truth is, rejection is good for you. It builds dedication and can make you committed to success if you let it. It gives you backbone and strengthens your resolve. Rejection can also inspire you to write more frequently, which allows you to improve your skills. All of this builds up your enthusiasm and motivates you to continue to work toward your dream. When you write and continue to pursue your goals despite rejection, your Writer Self-Image blossoms. You become more confident in your abilities. You grow in strength, courage, and resolve.

Rejection helps you overcome self-doubt because it forces you to draw upon your inner resources of motivation and dedication. When you hold that letter in your hand or read that e-mail, you have to say to yourself, "Just wait until they see my next story," or "I'll sell that book anyway."

This is the attitude that all writers who have gone on to find success have held toward rejection. "With every rejection letter that I got, and I got plenty, I was more determined to prove myself," says novelist Lori Foster. "It took me more than ten books and more than five years to make that first sale."

That's the kind of attitude you should have, too.

Rejection lets you know that you are making progress toward your writing goals; it's concrete proof that you are actively working toward your dream of becoming a successful writer. Sometimes rejection letters hold clues as to where you might improve; perhaps an editor or agent is impressed enough by your work to write a personal note back to you or to scribble a helpful line about where you could improve. I was once astonished to receive a two-page letter from an agent detailing what was wrong with my novel, *Grave Secret*. I incorporated many of her suggestions for improvement, and the book eventually sold.

Rejection can help you overcome self-doubt by solidifying your resolve to meet your Vision of Success *Plus* milestones. It inspires you to improve your skills. How? Read on.

Daily Direction

Write about how you overcame an obstacle in order to achieve a non–writing-related goal. Describe the obstacle and how you overcame it. What strengths do you possess that you can apply to overcoming self-doubt in your writing? Write about that. When you are done, move directly into your work-in-progress.

Use Rejection in Positive Ways

Receiving a rejection slip gives you the perfect opportunity to notice the thoughts and feelings you have about rejection and how these affect your behaviors. Here's what you can do. The next time a story or article idea of yours gets rejected, immediately take out your journal and make notes about what thoughts you are having regarding your abilities as a writer and the feelings those are generating. Try to identify the deep thoughts that may be causing you to harbor self-doubt. Notice any tendency to give up. Then turn those thoughts around and come up with replacements that make you feel empowered toward your writing goals.

Whenever you receive a rejection letter, you should make a special point of doing something toward your writing Vision of Success *Plus* within one day. Never let a rejection set you back, or stop you from writing, for more than twenty-four hours. Tell yourself that you will feel bad for one day, then feel bad, get it over with, and get right back in the saddle.

Activity: Your Writing Autobiography

You have already completed a major activity toward overcoming self-doubt in Chapter 3—you created a Vision of Success *Plus* and listed milestones that focus on all the steps that you can take now, today, to work toward your writing dream.

This exercise is similar to that one because it forces you to take the big picture and then narrow it down to one action that you can take right this minute to overcome self-doubt about your long-term writing goals. This is the exercise you will use whenever self-doubt is keeping you from writing.

The activity is simple. In your notebook, write a 400-word autobiography of the writing accomplishments that you hope to have achieved in about five years; refer back to your milestones from your Vision of Success *Plus* for inspiration. This autobiography should include books you want to have written, awards you want to win, and your future plans. If you need an example, pull down a few books by your favorite authors and look at their biographies on the book jackets. Then write something similar for yourself.

After you have completed this, list the ways that you have been letting self-doubt hold you back from achieving the desires outlined in this autobiography. Then, quickly and without giving it much thought, write down one activity that you could take right this instant to achieve that biography you just wrote. Whatever flashes into your mind, take that action immediately. It might be to write more often. It might be that you should attend a certain conference or submit your work to a particular magazine. Take the action that your subconscious mind suggests right away.

Keep your autobiography in a place where you can easily refer to it for inspiration and motivation as you move forward in your journey to become a successful writer.

Activity: Make a Self-Image Bulletin Board

In Chapter 2, I asked you to write down the reasons why you want to accomplish your writing goals as part of developing your Writer Self-Image. Remember that these reasons are usually where the motivation and dedication to achieve your goals reside. You can draw confidence from these reasons when self-doubt threatens to overwhelm you.

Novelist Amber Leigh Williams has a unique way of using her reasons to write—she turns them into a collage to help her get through periods of discouragement and self-doubt. "I have a bulletin board in my office and the images on it represent the reasons I began writing in the first place and where I would like to be in my writing career a year from now," she says. "It really helps to have that reassurance whenever that voice in my head starts niggling."

The images on Williams's board serve as instant reminders of why she is continuing to work toward success as a writer. But Williams uses more than her current goals to encourage her in the face of self-doubt—she also uses her one-year Vision of Success *Plus* milestones to inspire her collages, too. You can do the same. Create your own Writer Self-Image bulletin board that holds images of the reasons that you started writing in the first place and where you want to be in one, three, five, ten, and twenty years. Whenever you get stuck in your writing or that fear of failure settles into your chest as you think about sitting down to write, look at your Writer Self-Image bulletin board and allow the reasons you want to attain this self-image nudge you past your reticence. This is a great technique to help keep you on track and help you to write even in the face of self-doubt.

Live Your Life Write

The theory of self-sabotaging states that people will create an obstacle to success when they strongly desire success, but doubt their ability to achieve it. Self-doubt is usually related to fear: either fear of failure or fear of success. Creating obstacles to writing success takes many forms; one of the most common is simply to avoid writing. There are ways to manage self-doubt so that it does not have a negative impact on your writing. Some ways to combat self-doubt in your own writing life include:

- Entering contests as a way of practicing getting your work out there.
- Writing an autobiography of your desired writing accomplishments, then pinpointing one action you can take now to work toward making that biography a reality.
- Making a Writer Self-Image bulletin board, with pictures representing why you want to succeed as an author.
- Using rejection to your advantage by allowing it to strengthen your resolve.

Chapter 7

Mirror

Techniques

YOU MAY BE SURPRISED TO LEARN that you can use an ordinary mirror to help you overcome self-doubt, fear of failure, and low self-confidence when it comes to your writing endeavors. Using a mirror can even help you write every day. When put to specific uses like the ones we will discuss in this chapter, an ordinary mirror is transformed into a handy tool to have in your writer's toolbox. Whenever you deliberately use a mirror in the various ways that we will discuss in this chapter, you are able to appeal directly to your vast subconscious mind. A mirror helps you go directly to the source of your enthusiasm, motivation, and dedication for writing—your subconscious—and enlist its help in achieving all of your writing goals fast and easy.

You can basically use a mirror to build a bridge from your conscious to your subconscious mind. Think about it. Whenever you look directly into your own eyes in the mirror, don't you feel something like a pull in your solar plexus region (the tender place just above your abdomen)? I know I do. You are looking at yourself on a fundamentally deep level. You are getting in touch with your inner self. Using a mirror to speed up the realization of your writing dreams is an effective strategy for writers at all levels of their careers.

"Once I got clear with the specifics of my goal then I could put my effort and focus toward achieving it."

—Author Mary Buckham

Uses of a Mirror for Writers

Mirror techniques work because just having a mirror in the same room makes people more self-aware and more alert to their thoughts and feelings. Mirrors heighten your sense of self and make you more conscious of your behaviors and the motivations behind them. For example, one study found that people were less likely to be dishonest whenever a mirror was present in the environment.

Let's look at a few of the ways you can use the power of a mirror to help you write, build a bridge to your subconscious, and make your writing sessions more powerful.

As Motivation to Write

If you have chosen a writing schedule but consistently find that you fail to follow through on it, hang a mirror in your writing space. Hang it where you can see yourself whenever you sit down to write. The mirror will make you more alert to your own behavior in your writing space; you are less likely to simply sit and stare off into space when you can see yourself. The mirror will make you more cognizant of the fact that you should be writing at your chosen time. It will motivate you to follow through on your own promises to yourself because it will bring your behavior into your conscious awareness.

Improve Your Writer Self-Image Through Subconscious Impression

A writer writes. To keep reminding yourself of that simple fact, place a mirror on your writing desk so you can see your face as you write. This will serve to reinforce the impression of you in the act of writing on your subconscious mind, which will enhance your Writer Self-Image, boost your morale, and strengthen your confidence. As your Writer Self-Image improves, your motivation and dedication to achieve your writing goals becomes stronger; writing with a mirror on your desk sends a clear visual signal to your subconscious mind that you are indeed a writer because you can see yourself in the act of writing.

When you find yourself goofing off at your writing desk, turn to the mirror and look into your eyes. Remind yourself that you are a writer, and that writers write. Then return to your work in progress.

Daily Direction

If you are having trouble sitting down to write every day, buy an egg timer and set it for ten minutes. Begin writing and do not stop until the timer goes off. Repeat the exercise at least once.

Build a Bridge to Your Subconscious

Placing a mirror in your writing space can also help you access your subconscious mind more readily. Whenever you get stuck, look up into your own eyes in the mirror and ask whatever question has you stumped at the time. Gazing into your own eyes essentially poses the question to your subconscious mind. Take a few deep breaths, and allow your subconscious to prompt an answer into your conscious mind. With practice this technique becomes easier and more powerful.

Hill's Mirror Technique

A good method for programming your subconscious mind and bringing about your writing goals and Vision of Success *Plus* is to use the mirror technique created in the early 1900s by Napoleon Hill. Look in the mirror and make positive statements that pertain to your writing and your writing dreams several times per day.

For instance, if you want to earn a certain amount of money from writing, stand in front of a mirror, look into your eyes, and say something like, "I make five thousand dollars a month from writing." If you want to earn a certain amount on a book advance, state that. If you are having difficulty landing an agent, stand in front of your mirror every day and say, "Agents love my ideas and my manuscripts sell easily." If you need to improve your daily writing habit, stand in front of the mirror and state, "I am writing daily," or, "I write every day."

By declaring your writing goals and intentions to yourself in the mirror as if they were already a reality, you are effectively impressing those images on to your subconscious and helping to speed up the process of manifestation; in turn, your subconscious mind will nudge you to take actions every day that move you along toward achieving the intentions you have stated.

The Write Stuff

"Begin with the goal of writing for
thirty minutes a day. Meet this thirty-minute goal for a
week—then reward yourself."

—Author Cynthia Eden

Generate Enthusiasm and Positive Feelings

Another useful technique is to use a mirror to generate positive feelings within yourself. When you need to feel inspired about your writing, stand in front of the mirror, look into your eyes, and say "I feel inspired!" Say it with feeling, and mean it. When you want to feel enthusiastic say, "I feel enthusiastic!" To reach your writing goals, stand in front of the mirror and state your goals as if you had already achieved them—for example, "I wrote five pages today!" Notice how great it makes you feel to say that. You can use this method to achieve your Vision of Success *Plus* milestones, too. Look into your eyes and proclaim, "I sold my novel to my dream agent!"

You can use this technique anywhere. If you are in a public restroom, simply think your statements as you gaze at your reflection. Do it in your car using the rearview mirror when you're stopped at a traffic light. Carry a small mirror in your purse or briefcase and use the technique throughout the day. Anytime you find yourself in front of a mirror, reaffirm your goals and feelings of enthusiasm, motivation, and dedication to your writing dreams.

Reinforce Your Replacement Thoughts and "I" Statements

Take the positive replacement thoughts and the "I" statements that you have created in Chapters 1 and 5 and read those to yourself in front of your mirror. Look deeply into your eyes and believe the positive things you are saying to yourself, about yourself. Believing that these positive statements are already true makes you a more positive writer and stimulates your subconscious mind to help you find ways to achieve the goals you have set for yourself.

Avoid Self-Sabotage

Often people try subconscious programming techniques, but deep down, they do not believe the techniques will work for them. As with all techniques that involve programming the subconscious mind, it's important that you *feel* how you will really feel when the result is achieved as you state your proclamations in front of the mirror. Emotion is fuel to the subconscious and speeds up the process of creation. A negative attitude counteracts your efforts to make progress toward your goals because the subconscious mind responds to the dominant feeling of the conscious mind.

In other words, if you try the mirror techniques but are constantly thinking to yourself that they won't work for you, or that they are silly, and so on, then you are basically wasting your effort. It's important to harbor an attitude of open-mindedness and willingness to try. It helps to imagine in great detail the outcome of what you are striving to achieve and the feelings of success and joy that will come out of those accomplishments.

Activity: Mirror Practice

For at least one week, stand in front of the mirror in the morning and at night before you go to bed and state your goals, milestones, and other anticipated achievements with enthusiasm. Act as though these goals had already come to pass. Notice how you feel before, during, and after the process. Record it in your journal. Take careful notes about how the exercise impacts your thought-feeling-behavior cycle; do you find yourself more enthusiastic and motivated to complete your daily writing schedule? Do you feel recommitted to your writing goals and your Vision of Success *Plus*? You probably will. Use this newfound commitment as motivation to incorporate writing into your daily life and repeat this mirror technique on an ongoing basis to reinforce the subconscious programming needed to reach your goals.

Live Your Life Write

A mirror is an ordinary household item that, when used deliberately, can help you program your subconscious mind in a manner that positively impacts your thought-feeling-behavior cycle and helps you achieve writing success. Remember to:

- Use a mirror to program your subconscious mind to manifest your writing goals and Vision of Success *Plus*.
- Stand in front of a mirror every morning and night, look into your eyes, and state your goals with enthusiasm.
- Generate the feelings that you will have when you achieve your writing goals to add power to the programming statements you are feeding your subconscious.

Chapter 8

Role-Modeling

CHOOSING A SUCCESSFUL AUTHOR that you wish to emulate and using that person as a role-model from afar is a good strategy for finding success as a writer. Role-modeling an author you admire and whose success habits are similar to those that suit your lifestyle helps you define and hone in on success. Basically, role-modeling another successful author gives you a template to follow. It can help you stay on track with your writing goals, reinforce the habit of writing every day, and achieve your Vision of Success. It allows you to weave writing into your daily life by emulating a more successful author's writing habits. You can look at the way your role-model works and how she handles success and failure and use these as guideposts for your own writing and writing career.

Role-Modeling Is Different from Comparison

Role-modeling is not copying another person or trying to be their clone; it is simply using the qualities of a writer you admire as a touchstone to keep you moving ahead toward your own success. Role-modeling is fundamentally different from comparison.

Comparison holds a negative connotation and it puts you in a one down situation. When you compare yourself to someone else, you are typically only looking at all the ways that you believe you are not as good as or not as successful as the other person. In a comparison situation, the person doing the comparing always comes out on the short end of the stick. That is not the goal with role-modeling a successful author.

Role-modeling does not mean that you are trying to become an exact copy of another person and match his success step for step, or that you are trying to be or become someone other than yourself. That is unhealthy. You want to attain your own unique brand of success as a writer. Emulating another author that you admire is just a way to inspire yourself to keep pushing and moving ahead toward your Vision of Success, just as your role-model is pushing and moving ahead toward hers. You want to select traits and qualities that you admire and use those as a springboard for your own behaviors. You choose behaviors, attitudes, work habits, and other elements of another writer's life that might represent success in your own writing life and strive to emulate these things in your own way.

In the early stages of your career, role-modeling can help you because it provides you with positive behaviors, thoughts, and feelings that can guide you on your path to success. No one person knows everything, and with role-modeling you are simply following in the footsteps of someone further along the journey. You will put your own unique signature on the steps you choose.

Keep This in Mind

As we move ahead with the discussion of role-modeling, keep in mind that when you role-model someone that you do not personally know, you are essentially emulating an ideal. It's always easy to assume that a writer who has achieved success got there the easy way or did not have the kinds of obstacles or difficulties to overcome that you do. It is human nature to think that anyone who has achieved success of any sort is living a charmed life. But that is hardly ever the case, especially with writers. The obstacles that an author has overcome never show on the outside. When you read about another author's success, meet him at a conference, or attend one of her book signings, all you see is the glossy, finished exterior. You do not know what types of problems or setbacks that author had to get around in order to achieve his success.

The Write Stuff

"I love hearing other writers tell their stories. This was especially useful before I was published."

—Award-winning author Harley Jane Kozak

All successful authors have had to overcome what often seem like insurmountable problems in order to get where they are today. After interviewing more than 150 successful, bestselling writers, I can attest to this fact. The authors I have talked to have had to overcome the typical problems any writer faces such as rejection, struggling to find the right agent or publisher, and so forth, but many have also battled physical health problems, family issues, deaths, and personal demons. In my own life, it seems that every time I get a new book contract some crisis happens that acts as a major distraction to getting the book done in the already limited time I have to write. In fact, I reviewed the galley copies for my first two published books when I was ill and in a doctor's office hooked up to an IV.

Bestselling author CJ Lyons provides another example of the types of setbacks that can happen along the path to a successful writing career. "I had a phone call from a New York city editor who had read my first chapter and wanted to buy the book," she says. "The book ended up selling, received cover quotes and endorsements from a dozen bestsellers including Sandra Brown, and I of course was imagining my dream come true. Until 100 days prior to publication the book was pulled because of cover art problems. Suddenly there I was with no book. And I had just left my pediatric practice to write full time and support myself with my writing. Suddenly I had no job, no prospects for income, no agent, and no idea what to do, except keep on writing."

Still, Lyons pressed forward with her goals and marched steadily along toward her Vision of Success, and today she is the author of four bestselling novels. Lyons's story represents a good example that you might use for role-modeling because now that you know her story, you might choose to emulate her persistence and tenacity as she continued writing in the face of a crushing disappointment.

Many Uses of Role-Modeling

There are a number of ways that you can use role-modeling to reach your writing goals. You can emulate your favorite author's writing schedule. You can investigate how your role-model overcame obstacles that you are currently facing and use his example to find a way around your own blockage. One of the best uses of role-modeling is for inspiration; when you become discouraged with your writing process, reviewing your role-model's story of success can sometimes be all it takes to get you back on track with your own work-in-progress. Let's look at each strategy individually.

Role-Modeling Helps You Write

Looking at the writing habits of authors you admire can motivate you to implement those habits in your writing life. For instance, I used role-modeling when I first realized that I wanted to become a writer. I got the idea to get up early, before dawn, and write for a few hours before work after reading that Alice Koller, the author of *An Unknown Woman* and other memoirs, rose at 4:30 A.M. to write for several hours before beginning her day.

When learning how to write fiction, I role-modeled authors I wished to emulate by typing out some of the text from their books as a way to get an organic feel for how they write, the words they choose, scene structure, dialogue, and so forth. This is a technique I still sometimes turn to; it stimulates my creative flow and inspires me to get back to my own work-in-progress in no time.

Role-modeling a successful author's writing habits is a useful tool for writers at any stage of their career. The actual task of writing can be a lonely process. Only you can write your books, and only you can sit down at your desk and get the words on the page. It's nice to have the support of other writers, even from afar, as you move along your solitary path.

Daily Direction

Begin your daily writing session with a dose of inspiration from your favorite author.
Read a chapter from one of her novels as motivation to write your own story.

Role-modeling Helps You Overcome Obstacles

Napoleon Hill repeatedly discussed the idea that whenever you set out on a path to meet any goal, you should expect obstacles, delays, and difficulties. He stated that the bigger the goal, the more problems you should anticipate having as you work toward achieving it.

Role-modeling gives you a way to look at other writers who have gone before you and make a plan for overcoming anticipated obstacles, delays, and difficulties. For example, knowing that you will have unexpected problems spring up when you begin working toward a goal gives you a heads up that experiencing hurdles is a normal part of achieving success. Some problems you can plan for, such as rejection. It's common knowledge that rejection is part of the business of being a writer. Even people who don't want to be writers know this. Just look at every writer who has ever been published; they were all rejected at one point or another, some of them hundreds of times. So you can use this information to mentally prepare yourself for your own rejection. This does not mean that rejection doesn't hurt or isn't disappointing; it just means that when you plan for and expect to get rejected as part of your journey toward becoming a successful author, you can make plans as to how to get around it. Making plans for overcoming a hurdle is the key to navigating it. Looking at how the authors you want to emulate handle rejection gives you a touchstone for moving past your own.

The Write Stuff

"I can share mistakes I've made in the hopes that others can avoid them. I can share feelings I had so that others might better understand them when they're faced with the same emotional upheavals. And I can share advice, given from experience."

—Novelist Lori Foster

Reading as Role-Modeling Provides Inspiration

One of the greatest benefits of role-modeling is that it gives you inspiration to pursue your long-term writing goals over time, and reading the books of authors you wish to emulate is a good way to get this inspiration when you feel your own enthusiasm flagging; an added benefit is that you are absorbing the craft of writing at the same time.

Reading other writers she wishes to emulate is a strategy that novelist Anna Hackett uses to keep going in her own career. "Reading a fabulous book that grabs me by the throat and leaves me thinking about the characters days later always motivates me to do the same in my stories," she says.

Reading helps novelist Cynthia Eden stay inspired and dedicated to achieving her own writing goals. "Over the years, I was able to maintain my focus simply by reading," she says. "Whenever I had doubt I just picked up a book, read it, and realized once again—this is what I want to do. Sometimes, just walking into a bookstore would rejuvenate me."

Reading her own published books is a success strategy for award-winning author Nancy Martin. "I'm a big believer in the power of reading. It's magic sometimes," she says. "I've even been known to read some of my own books. After a couple of pages, I usually think to myself, 'Hey, I'm not so bad after all!' Often, a single word or phrase will trigger the creative process for me again."

Using reading as role-modeling is a way to regain your motivation and dedication to succeed at your own writing goals. It's a strategy that has worked for me, too. I have been known to re-read the books on my "keeper shelf" as a way to not only learn the craft of writing but also to immerse myself in the one thing that inspires me to write more than anything else—the pleasure of losing myself in a well-written book. Knowing how difficult good writing can be, I appreciate how much hard work my favorite authors put into their stories, and I am always inspired to do the same.

Applying Role-Modeling to Your Writing Life

There are many ways to use role-modeling to help your own career as a writer. You can choose traits from several different authors that you admire to incorporate into your daily routine. You can also emulate habits that have worked well for someone else's career path. The nice thing about role-modeling is that it is an eclectic and unique process; you can pick and choose the things about many different authors that will work well in your own life to help you achieve your own unique brand of success.

Now that you see how role-modeling can help you attain your own writing success, let's look at two specific strategies for applying it to your life: creating an ideal writer and an ideal composite writer.

Your Ideal Writer

You have an ideal Writer Self-Image that you are working to attain. This Writer Self-Image is made up of certain habits and traits that, in your mind, define you as an ideal writer. A good way to use the technique of role-modeling to help you achieve this image is to pick an author you wish to emulate and make a list of the traits, qualities, and behaviors that you think they display on a regular basis and then work to do the same.

To do this, simply choose an author who you admire and, in your notebook, write down what you think the writing habits are that have allowed her to attain success. A good place to find this type of information is the author's website. Most authors have a biography listed on their home page where they share some of the details of their struggles and how they got published. Use that biography to make a list of the writing habits that the author likely displayed on their road to success. If the author has written an autobiography or a craft book on writing, read it. You want to be as accurate as possible with your traits list; however, it is important to note that you can still use the technique even if you aren't 100 percent correct or can't find highly detailed information about your role-model. The goal here is simply for you to create a working range of actions that can guide your own behaviors as you work toward your Vision of Success. Remember, you are not trying to copy exactly how someone else did it or become his clone; you simply want to set some general guidelines that can steer your own behavior. So jot down some thoughts on how you believe this author achieved his success based on the information you can find about him.

Daily Direction

If you are having difficulty making writing part of your daily routine, choose an author who writes every day as your role-model. Each time you feel resistant to focusing on your own work-in-progress, ask yourself what your role-model would do in that situation.

Let me give you an example of how successful authors implement this specific strategy. Several years ago I attended a large writing conference in Dallas. Many attendees were wearing buttons with WWND? inscribed on them. I asked what the acronym stood for and was told it meant "What would Nora do?", meaning what would bestselling author Nora Roberts do. These button wearing aspiring authors were using the ideal of Nora Roberts as a touchstone for their own behaviors and actions as they strove toward their own writing success. For instance, when they did not feel like writing, the button reminded them to ask themselves what Nora Roberts would do when she didn't feel like writing. The answer of course is that she probably writes no matter how she feels. What would Nora Roberts do if she were nervous about pitching a manuscript idea to an editor at a conference? She would probably do it nervous. What does Nora Roberts do to bring the craft of writing into her daily life? The answer is that she makes writing a priority every day. And so forth.

In a similar way, when you are working to pick an author you admire, ask yourself "What would Author X do?" It's a good way to stay focused on your daily writing goals while motivating and inspiring yourself to keep working toward your long-term goals.

A Composite Ideal Writer

Another way to use role-modeling to attain your own writing success is to create an ideal composite writer. You probably have several authors who you admire; some you may have even met at conferences or book signings. Creating a composite ideal writer is a useful strategy. You simply combine the traits and habits that these successful authors possess and strive to emulate those.

One way to create an ideal composite writer is to attend conferences and listen closely to the keynote speaker or attend an author's workshop and listen for clues about how she succeeded. As with role-modeling a single author, you can check various websites and pull together the biographies of several writers you admire. You can also subscribe to author's blogs or read profiles on successful authors in writing magazines as a way to gain insight into their writing habits and their thoughts, feelings, and behaviors with respect to writing.

Attending many conferences and absorbing information from published writers is a strategy that worked for award-winning author Harley Jane Kozak before she was published. "I would go to conferences and seminars and listen and listen and eventually the message sunk in: the only difference between the published and the pre-published is that published writers kept doing it and didn't give up," she says. "They write every day, or most days, they send out their work, they deal with rejection, they write some more, send it out again, and so on."

This strategy can work for you, too. Perhaps you learned that Author X writes Monday through Friday and takes weekends off to be with her family. So the habit of writing five days per week would be something that you want to incorporate into your composite writer role-model. Maybe you have read that Author Y was rejected 300 times before he sold his first novel. The traits that you would want to list on your ideal composite might be persistence, tenacity, or believing in one's self. In another author's autobiography, you read that she prefers rewriting to writing first drafts, whereas a stumbling block for you is that you typically get frustrated when your first drafts aren't perfect and you give up on the manuscript. For obvious reasons, you want to change this habit. The trait you could list for your ideal composite writer might be "accepts imperfection on first drafts" or "loves rewriting." Whatever would help you learn to enjoy rewriting is what you should list for your ideal composite role-model.

This ideal composite represents the type of writer you trying to become. It gives you a springboard to use as a jumping off point for your own success by guiding and directing your thoughts, feelings, and behavior. This version of role-modeling is a great tool because it allows you to take traits and habits from several writers and incorporate those into your own writing lifestyle.

Remember that you are not comparing yourself to these other writers. You are simply pulling clues about how they achieved their success from what you know about them.

Role-modeling is a useful way to gain insight and understanding into what it takes to become a successful author and to provide yourself with a working image of success; it gives you a template to use as a guide for your own thoughts, feelings, and actions. In the next chapter, we'll discuss the concept of Image Incorporation, an extension of role-modeling that can lead you to even greater success.

Activity: Create Your Ideal Role-Model

In this activity, you will create a role-model. Choose one author or several authors whom you admire and whose work habits and traits you wish to emulate; then list the habits, traits, attitudes, and behaviors that you know or believe this writer or writers display. You may find it helpful to reference the biographies of the authors quoted in this book; all of their websites are included in the appendix. Some questions you might ask yourself to get to these various attributes include:

- What type of writing schedule does this writer have? *Examples of successful author schedules: daily writing, five days per week, all day on Saturday, every night after the family is in bed.*
- How does this writer handle rejection? *Examples of how successful authors handle rejection: brush it off, use it to improve their skills, see it as a necessary part of becoming successful.*
- What does this writer do when she loses interest in or becomes frustrated with her work-in-progress? *Examples of successful author responses: keep moving forward, write through the frustration, take a break and then come back to it, talk to another writer for encouragement.*
- What does this writer do when she doesn't feel like writing? *Examples of successful author responses: write anyway, set a self-imposed deadline, review their Vision of Success, reread their goals, read other writers for inspiration, join a critique group for support.*
- What does this writer do when he feels nervous about submitting his work? *Examples of successful author responses: practice the mirror technique to build self-confidence, review the emotional reasons why he wants to complete his writing goals, imagine himself submitting his work despite feeling nervous, submit anyway.*

From this list of questions and answers, and you may have more, cull a list of work habits, attitudes, traits, thoughts, feelings, and behaviors that your role-model displays. Write this list on a separate sheet of paper and hang it next to your Vision of Success, or someplace else where you will see it every day as a way of reminding yourself what you need to do, think, and feel in order to achieve your own writing success.

Live Your Life Write

Role-modeling is a practical and easy-to-implement technique for finding success as a writer. You are using another person's work habits, traits, and attributes as a guide for your own behavior so that you can achieve your own unique success. Remember:

- Role-modeling is not copying or trying to be a clone of another person. It is emulating the thoughts, feelings, and behaviors of authors you admire into your own writing habits so that you can achieve your own writing goals in your own way.
- You can create an ideal writer or an ideal composite writer by studying successful authors' biographies, reading profiles about them in writing magazines, attending their workshops at conferences, or attending their book signings.
- When you get discouraged or don't feel like writing, ask yourself what your favorite author would do in that situation, and then do the same thing.

Chapter 9

Image

Incorporation

IN THE LAST CHAPTER YOU LEARNED ABOUT ROLE-MODELING: what it is and how it can help you achieve success as a writer. Here, we will take the concept of role-modeling a step further and discuss Image Incorporation, an easy technique that allows you to absorb, at a subconscious level, the useful habits and traits that you have identified from your role-models so you can manifest those traits on a deep level in your own writing life. Image Incorporation helps you to grow into the image of your ideal writer and take on success-oriented habits faster than using the role-modeling process alone. Image Incorporation is a way to capitalize on the power of your subconscious mind because you are programming it to help you display success oriented traits and habits in your daily writing life.

What Is Image Incorporation?

Image Incorporation is a sound psychological exercise that allows people to program the traits and habits of another person into their own subconscious minds in order to overcome obstacles and achieve personal growth. Psychologists first used this practice as a way to help people overcome negative habits and traits and replace them with more positive, beneficial ones. For you, this technique allows you to actually absorb some of the qualities of the writers you admire on a subconscious level, which in turn, helps you achieve even greater control over your thoughts, feelings, and behaviors as you strive to emulate their positive traits. As with role-modeling, you are not attempting to copy or become the clone of another person. You are simply taking the traits, attributes, and habits of a successful author that you admire and programming your subconscious mind to help you display those same traits in order to achieve your own brand of success. You are essentially absorbing your role-model's success-oriented mind-set at a subconscious level in order to positively influence your own writing habits.

The Write Stuff

"I read the early biographies of writers I admired, and stories about their struggles before they were published."

—Author Barbara O'Neal

Image Incorporation is a tool that many successful authors use to attain their own goals and become better writers—both before and after publication. As a new author, Mary Buckham was surprised and humbled to discover that even *New York Times* bestsellers still strive to learn from other writers. Now, she does the same thing. "I remember walking into a workshop one day and in the front row were five, and I counted them twice, five multiple *New York Times* authors sitting there, leaning forward, ready to learn," she says. "I think of those writers often and silently thank them for showing me a path."

Writing and learning the craft of writing is an ever expanding upward spiral, and you will never stop learning and growing. Having role-models who are further along the path than you are to inspire and motivate you to keep growing is what Image Incorporation is all about.

Keep a writing notebook at your breakfast table. As you are drinking your coffee in the morning, write a few paragraphs about your work-in-progress: where you are in the story, how your progress has been to date, where you want to go with the material. This gets your mind thinking about the daily writing and allows your subconscious to begin priming your creative pump. When you sit down to write that day, you will get into the writing session more easily.

Steps to Image Incorporation

There are four steps to successfully using the Image Incorporation process:

- choose your role-model
- write your subconscious mind programming statements
- visualize
- act

Please note that Image Incorporation is not an instantaneous process. Subconscious mind programming takes time and effort. You will not do this activity one time and suddenly display the positive writing habits and traits of your admired author or composite author. You will want to plan on using the Image Incorporation exercise at least twice per week, even more if you can, for at least four weeks to achieve maximum results. This technique is an ongoing process. You will also want to keep your programming statements handy, so that you can read them every day. This will reinforce the programming process. Most importantly, you will want to *act* every day in ways that support the positive Writer Self-Image you are striving to create.

Now let's discuss an actual Image Incorporation example so that you can easily use the activity at home for your own success.

The Write Stuff

"I studied the books I loved to figure out 'How did that author do X so well?'"

—*New York Times* bestselling author Dianna Love

Step One: Choose Your Role-Model

This is the author or the ideal composite author you admire who has traits, attributes, and work habits similar to those you wish to incorporate into your daily writing habits to achieve your own success. You got a head start with this step by identifying your role-model in the last chapter.

Example

I will use as my role-model an author that I admire: *New York Times* bestselling author Sherrilyn Kenyon. As you already know, the first step in Image Incorporation is to collect as much information as you can about the author you wish to emulate. I already gave you some ways to do this: read their autobiographies, read their biographies on their websites, find magazine articles written about them, read their blogs, go to conferences where they are speaking, attend their book signings, and so forth.

In this case, my editor had arranged for me to interview Ms. Kenyon, so I am fortunate to have first hand information on her work habits as well as some of her attributes and traits related to writing. I had also read her biography on her website, and I recently heard her tell the story of challenges she overcame to become a successful author at a writing conference where she was the keynote speaker and I was an attendee.

From that conference speech, I know that Ms. Kenyon overcame huge obstacles to earn the success she has today. I know that she had to hold on to her writing dream through abject poverty and scathing rejections where she was told that no publishing house in New York wanted to develop her and that she should stop submitting her material for consideration. From my interview with her, I know that Ms. Kenyon writes every day. I know that she has hundreds of stories batting around inside her head, and she is compelled by her Burning Desire to Write to get those stories on to paper. I know that she constantly gets new ideas, that she can write anywhere, including while watching her kids play soccer, and that she carries her work-in-progress so that if an unexpected opportunity arises, she can sit down and write.

From this information on Ms. Kenyon, the habits, traits, and attributes that I wish to incorporate into my own Writer Self-Image include:

- Write every day
- Write anywhere, any time
- Persistence
- Get lots of ideas for stories
- Keep writing despite rejections to achieve writing dream
- Write prolifically

Step Two: Write Subconscious Programming Statements

This is the process where you take the habits and traits of your role-model and turn these into programming statements for your subconscious mind.

Example

Now that I have a list of Ms. Kenyon's writing habits, attributes, and traits that I want to incorporate into my Writer Self-Image, I will write programming statements to feed these success habits and traits into my subconscious mind. As I mentioned before, write your programming statements before you use the guided meditation exercise on the accompanying CD, since your programming statements will be unique to you. You want to feed your subconscious mind the specific traits that you wish to emulate and end with the phrase, "… like my role-model, Author X." Stating the person's name gives your subconscious mind a clear picture of what you are trying to accomplish and strengthens the programming process. This also allows you to use different traits and habits from different authors.

Below are examples of the programming statements I will use based on the information I have about Sherrilyn Kenyon. Please note that when you program your subconscious mind, you address it directly. The examples below illustrate how to do this. Some examples of subconscious mind programming statements that I will use include:

- Subconscious, help me to write every day like Sherrilyn Kenyon.
- Subconscious, help me to be able to write anywhere and any time like Sherrilyn Kenyon.
- Subconscious, help me to develop the persistence of Sherrilyn Kenyon so that I can achieve my own writing dreams.
- Subconscious, help me to keep writing through rejections like Sherrilyn Kenyon did so that I can become a successful author.

Again, if you have more than one author whose habits and traits you wish to incorporate into your own image, that's fine. Simply create a programming statement for that habit or trait and use the person's name at the end so your subconscious mind has an image to attach to the statement. For example, I know from my interviews with *New York*

Times bestselling author Dianna Love that she works on as many as three book projects at a time. If I wanted to emulate that writing habit, I would program my subconscious with a statement like, "Subconscious, help me work on more than one book at a time like Dianna Love." I know from reading Stephen King's autobiography, *On Writing*, that he writes every day except major holidays. If this was a habit I wanted to incorporate into my Writer Self-Image, I would use the statement, "Subconscious, help me to write every day like Stephen King."

Step Three: Visualize

After you have completed the programming process, use visualization to deepen the programming. Visualization involves imagining yourself emulating the success habits of your role-model author in the manner you want to occur in your daily life.

Example

After I complete the programming statements, I will stay in the meditation and visualize myself thinking, feeling, and behaving in the ways that my new image supports. I will visualize myself getting lots of ideas like Sherrilyn Kenyon. I will visualize myself writing every day like Sherrilyn Kenyon. I will visualize myself writing anywhere and at any time like Sherrilyn Kenyon. I will visualize myself overcoming rejection like Sherrilyn Kenyon. If I am using the composite role-model, then I will visualize myself writing every day like Stephen King. I will visualize myself working on multiple book projects at once like Dianna Love. And so forth.

Again, the reason you want to use the image of your role-model in your visualization is to give your subconscious mind a concrete example of what you are trying to achieve. If one of your statements is that you will write every day like your favorite author, visualize yourself doing so. If a new attribute you want to incorporate is confidence, visualize yourself acting in a confident manner in a writing-related situation of your choosing just like your favorite author.

Step Four: Act!

Once you have completed the Image Incorporation exercise, you will want to come out of the guided meditation and move directly into a writing session. This will reinforce the positive writing habits that you are striving to create or strengthen.

Example

Now I put the programming into action! When I come out of the meditation, I will take action immediately that supports my new Writer Self-Image and the positive habits, traits, and attributes that I have absorbed from my role-model author. I will go immediately to my desk to write. I will create a running list of story ideas. I might begin keeping my laptop with me more, so that I can sit down and write anywhere, and anytime, like my role-model Sherrilyn Kenyon. When I get a rejection letter, I will toss it in a trash bin and keep on writing like Sherrilyn Kenyon, and so forth.

Activity: Reinforcing Your Programming Statements

Once again, write your programming statements on cards or in your journal so that you can read them every day. This will strengthen the subconscious programming process. Dwell on your programming statements as you move through your day. You can repeat them to yourself as you sit in traffic, while you wait for your lunch to arrive, when you first awaken, and before going to sleep at night. As you do so, visualize yourself acting in ways that manifest your new Writer Self-Image according to your role-model.

You should also plan to use the guided meditation exercise at least twice a week for at least one month when you first start the

Image Incorporation process. After that, strive to complete the exercise at least once a week until you notice positive changes in your behavior. Use the exercise periodically thereafter as a refresher.

Activity: Incorporate Those Images!

In your journal, go back to your notes on the role-model that you completed in Chapter 8 and choose the habits, traits, and attributes of your role-model or composite role-model that you wish to incorporate into your Writer Self-Image.

Next, create programming statements for your subconscious mind following the examples I gave earlier. Remember to address your subconscious mind directly. After you have completed five to seven programming statements, record these into your tape or digital recorder. Speak in a slow, clear voice, and repeat each statement twice, pausing for about a minute in between statements so that you can use the visualization process. As with all the exercises on the CD, find a comfortable place in your home where you will not be disturbed for about thirty minutes, dim the lights, turn off your cell phone, and get into a relaxed position. Turn on the CD and listen to the Image Incorporation track, playing your programming statements when prompted. As you hear the statements, visualize yourself acting in the ways that your role-model(s) act to achieve their writing success.

When you are finished with the CD, get up and go directly to your desk and write. You can focus on your work-in-progress, write about your experience with Image Incorporation, document any insights you had during the exercise, make a list of story ideas, create goals or milestones for your Vision of Success *Plus*, and so forth. Any activity related to the craft of writing should follow your Image Incorporation exercise to reinforce the programming statements.

Live Your Life Write

Image Incorporation is a tested, four-step psychological practice that helps you absorb beneficial habits and traits at a subconscious level. Remember to:

- Choose your role-model or a composite role-model.
- Make a list of habits, traits, and attributes of your role-model(s) that you wish to emulate and absorb into your own Writer Self-Image.
- Write your programming statements, addressing your subconscious mind directly and noting your role-model's name to give the subconscious a concrete image to work with.
- Visualize yourself acting in ways that support your new Writer Self-Image.
- Take action immediately to reinforce the programming statements and solidify your new Writer Self-Image. Use the Image Incorporation guided exercise at least twice a week for at least one month when you first begin the process, shifting to once per week thereafter until you notice the changes in your writing habits that you want to see.

Chapter 10

Acting

As

If

ACTING AS IF is based on Alfred Adler's principles of social psychology. Adler postulated that people draw conclusions about themselves through observation of their behavior just as they draw conclusions about other people based on observation of their behavior.

Out of this theory sprang the idea of Acting As If, the idea that if a person acts in the ways they want to become, they will gradually assume those traits over time. This concept fits nicely with the role-modeling process from Chapter 8 and the Image Incorporation that you started working on in Chapter 9. Once you get your Image Incorporation down pat, you simply act a certain way based on your ideal Writer Self-Image, and over time, you *become* what you are acting. Acting As If helps you develop and nurture the traits that will help you grow into the writer you want to be.

Throughout this chapter, we'll be looking at a variety of common traits that you can improve upon by use the Acting As If principle. You may have additional traits, attributes, and habits that you want to address. Whatever you want to make yourself believe about yourself as a writer, you can use the Acting As If theory to help you achieve.

How *Acting As If* Impacts Your Thought-Feeling-Behavior Cycle

Acting As If works because when you act in certain ways, even when you don't feel that way, over time you change your mental constructs or belief systems about yourself. For instance, if you act confident even when you don't feel confident, eventually your behavior programs your subconscious mind to believe that you are confident and so you become confident over time.

Remember that the thought-feeling-behavior cycle is circular, meaning you can impact any element of it and have an effect on the other two. Acting as if targets the behavior component of the cycle to bring about change in your thoughts and feelings.

Acting As If in Practice

You are probably already using the theory of Acting As If in your daily life. Think back to a time when you were afraid to do something but you did it anyway. Perhaps it was giving a presentation in front of your coworkers. Maybe you were asked to give a speech at your local Chamber of Commerce regarding your business. Or maybe you finally mustered the courage to send out that query letter to a national magazine that had been languishing in your word processor for six months.

How did you feel after you had completed your intimidating task? I'm willing to bet you felt pretty good. Even if it didn't go exactly as you had hoped it would, you likely still felt braver, more confident, and proud when it was all over. More importantly, the next time you were faced with doing something that made you nervous, whether it was a similar activity or not, you were probably more willing to do it. You had learned, through observation of your own behavior, that you could do something scary and live through it, and be successful at it as well. Your behavior influenced your thoughts and feelings directly. You didn't feel brave but you did it and so you must be brave after all. You didn't feel confident but you did it and so you must be confident after all. And so forth.

That's the theory of Acting As If in practice. You take on a trait that you do not possess but act as if you do possess it; you then behave in a way that demonstrates the trait and you observe yourself acting in this way. This in turn leads you to have the feelings that are connected to that trait.

The Acting As If theory says that when you observe yourself doing something you draw conclusions about yourself much as you do when you observe others. In this way, Acting As If shapes and changes your behavior over time and leads you to believe and feel that you possess whatever trait you are *acting as if*.

Make-Believe = Making Yourself Believe

Acting as if is a powerful way to nurture the success-oriented traits of your ideal Writer Self Image and begin completing tasks toward accomplishing your writing goals. It's a good way to extend your Image Incorporation exercises into your daily routine. A fun way to think of it is that it's like playing make-believe. When you pretend, you are *making yourself believe* that you are what you are pretending to be. You get to pretend that you already are a successful author, whatever that means to you, which will eventually lead to you becoming that successful author.

Acting As If You Are Confident

Acting as if you are confident in your writing, your writing abilities, and your writing future will help you make huge leaps toward actually getting to your Vision of Success. Why? Because you are changing your mental belief system. You are acting in ways that positively influence your thought-feeling-behavior cycle. When you act confident, you feel confident. When you feel confident, you begin having new thoughts and new beliefs about yourself that tell you that yes, you can do this. This in turn causes you to act in ways that a confident person would behave, and a confident you gradually emerges. Here are some tools to help you act as if you are a confident writer.

The Write Stuff

"I am the CEO of my own career and no successful CEO asks themselves, 'How do I feel today about my work?' They just do it."

—Author Mary Buckham

Compartmentalize Your Fear

One of the tricks that counselors often give people for combating fear and worry is to compartmentalize those emotions temporarily. You do this by visualizing the things that you are worried about being filed into a cabinet, a locking safe, or any other container. Close them up for safekeeping, and then proceed with your task. This sets aside worry and fear temporarily and allows your mind to focus on other, more productive tasks.

This can be a helpful tool for writers, too. When you find yourself doing something that elicits fear or nervousness within you, take a deep breath and shut away your worries in a mental filing cabinet. For example, let's say an editor sends you an e-mail saying he wants to discuss the query letter you sent in a month ago and to please call him as soon as possible. Coming across as confident will be important on the phone call, and yet because of your nervousness you fear you'll find yourself tongue-tied. To act as if you are confident, lock away your anxiety in the filing cabinet and pretend that you are feeling confident and positive. Visualize your nervousness as something meaningful to you—a word, a black cloud, a swarm of angry bees—and shut it away in the drawer for safekeeping. (You can let it back out once the phone call is over.)

Another trick is to visualize a giant mental hand shoving aside doubt, fear, and nervousness to create a clear path for you to move ahead. Simply visualize all your fear piling up on the side, out of your mental sight, and proceed with your task with a renewed sense of calm.

Be Prepared

One part of *acting as if* you are confident is to prepare yourself with any knowledge or information you might need before you go into a situation where you are nervous. It is my experience that the source of a lot of anxiety is often simply not having enough information. When you do not have enough information, you speculate. You start to make things up, and those things are usually a lot worse than the reality of the situation. Getting the facts straight can help you act as if you are confident because information gives you confidence.

Several years ago, I found myself consumed with anxiety before I gave my first pitch to an editor at a writing conference. I had never done it before and had no idea what I was doing or what to expect. So I prepared. I talked to other writers who had experience with giving pitches. I got advice on how to formulate a pitch and what to expect from the agent. After I had armed myself with the cognitive knowledge, I practiced my three-minute elevator pitch several times in front of a mirror. I practiced making eye contact, speaking clearly, and smiling.

The practice paid off. When it was my turn with the agent, I stood up straight, plastered a huge smile on my face, and walked into the room as if I owned the place. Inside I was quaking, but outside I was the picture of confidence. I acted as if I had given hundreds of pitches before. Within a few minutes of *acting as if* I were the most self-assured person on the planet, I began to calm down. I relaxed and actually enjoyed the process. When I left, I had learned something very important about myself—that I do okay under pressure when I use the Acting As If technique. You can, too.

Acting As If You Are Self-Motivated

Acting as if you are self-motivated is a bit of a misnomer because in reality, you already are self-motivated or you would not be reading this book. Self-motivated writers are continually looking for ways to improve themselves and their lives and attain new heights in their writing.

The problem a lot of aspiring writers have is putting that self-motivation into practice. Motivation is the thing that drives you to your desk, day after day, even when there is no outward sign of progress toward your long-term goal. Using the Acting As If technique to pretend that you are highly self-motivated can help draw your innate motivation out. Let's look at some ways that you can put the Acting As If principle into practice to strengthen your motivation.

Daily Direction

Take advantage of the power of small steps. Each week for a month, list on an index card one success-oriented writing habit you intend to act as if you already possess. Carry the card with you and make hash marks each time you successfully accomplish the habit. Try to increase the number of hash marks each day of the week.

How Bad Do You Want It?

When I first began writing ten years ago, I had no publication credits and no idea what I was doing. All I knew was that I had dreamed of becoming a writer all my life and I was inspired to act on that dream after reading the true life stories of successful people throughout history.

What I discovered is that all of these people were driven to succeed by some unknown inner source, and that they had worked for years—sometimes decades!—before they achieved any recognition or outward signs of accomplishment; they were internally driven and motivated to succeed.

I decided to act as if I were one of these highly driven people who were strongly motivated to succeed. I started getting up at 3:30 A.M. every day and writing for two hours before I went to my job. I did this every day of the week for many years without getting a single publication credit. There were times when I felt deeply discouraged. Sometimes it seemed like the rejection letters materialized in my mailbox faster than I mailed the queries.

What helped motivate me during these times of no visible progress was asking myself, "How bad do you want it?" Every time that alarm clock went off at 3:30 A.M. and I had to get up and chase what felt like a ghost of a dream, my answer when I asked myself "How bad do you want it?" was that I wanted to become a published, successful author very badly. In fact, there was nothing else I wanted more than that. Asking myself this question stirred the embers of my Burning Desire to Write; it reminded me of what I was working for. It helped me dig deep and dredge up the motivation to get out of that bed in what so often felt like the middle of the night and trudge off to my computer. In short, asking myself "How bad do you want it?" helped me act as if I were already a published, working author.

Ask yourself the question: How bad do I want to achieve my writing goals? You probably want it as much as I did. Use that to help you act as if you are motivated to keep working toward your Vision of Success.

Keep Your Writing to Yourself

One of the hazards of talking about your work-in-progress too much is that it can weaken your resolve to write it; after all, if you have told someone the story, what's the point in writing it down?

Keeping your stories to yourself until they are finished helps you act as if you are motivated to finish the book. This is a strategy that novelist Lori Foster uses. "I don't tell others about the book, and definitely not about the plot, because I think that weakens the resolve to write," she explains. "I share my stories after they're published, and not before, and that keeps me motivated to get it on paper and get it sent it off to the editor."

The Write Stuff

"To get back into the story groove, it helps me to reread a previous chapter. Once I'm at the point where I get pulled back into the story, the time flies by as I write new content."

—Author Annette Fix

This is not to say that you should not discuss your work with your critique group, at a workshop with other writers, or with another aspiring writer who is helping you improve your craft. But it's a good idea not to talk about your writing at work, or when dining out with friends, and so forth. Doing so takes some of the excitement for writing away and drains off some of the magic of the creative process.

Acting as if you are a self-motivated writer and making the conscious decision to write your story down instead of telling it to others influences your thought-feeling-behavior cycle because when you act motivated, you feel motivated and you think motivating statements. When you are finished writing for the day, you feel confident and happy and your thinking is positive, which increases the chances that you will follow through again tomorrow.

Acting As If You Are Self-Disciplined

Self-discipline is the Achilles heel for many aspiring writers. It is closely tied to motivation; when you are self-disciplined, you naturally display motivation, and vice versa. But many aspiring writers struggle with the necessary self-discipline that is needed over the course of many years to attain their writing dreams. *Acting as if* can help.

Finish Each Project

A key action that can help you act your way into feeling and being more self-disciplined is to finish every manuscript you start, no matter how much you start to hate it and no matter how bad you think it is. Even if you decide that you will shove it in a closet when you're finished and never show it to a single person—finish it. This is a critical strategy for building self-discipline that novelist Debra Webb uses. "I finish each project I start," she says. "Finishing is, in my opinion, a top priority. Whether a project ever sells or not, completing it makes you a better writer. It's exercise!"

To *act as if* you are a self disciplined writer, make a commitment that you will finish every manuscript you start. Doing so will strengthen your resolve to your writing goals.

Exercise Self-Discipline

The only way to have self-discipline is to exercise it. That means working your writing schedule whether you feel like it or not, and completing your daily word or page count goal whether you feel like it or not.

When you see yourself becoming undisciplined, use the Acting As If technique to act like a self-disciplined writer. Use your role-modeling exercises to remind yourself what your favorite authors do when they feel undisciplined and act as if you are that self-disciplined author who finishes what she starts, one day and one page at a time.

Acting As If You are Future Focused

Becoming a future-focused writer means always reaching up, toward your next goal. The nature of goals and achieving goals is such that once you accomplish something, you naturally want to press forward and challenge yourself to reach the next rung on your ladder. Moving onward and upward is a key strategy that many successful authors use to act their way into becoming future focused.

Visualize Goals as a Ladder

I often use a staircase analogy when talking about goals; your Vision of Success is at the top and you start on the bottom step and work your way up through your milestones, one step at a time. Future-focused writers understand that leaping to the top of the staircase is impossible. They focus on one small goal at a time, each one progressively closer to their Vision of Success at the top of the stairs.

Another analogy that works is to visualize a ladder. Each rung on the ladder represents a goal. In order to climb to the top, you have to step on the lowest rung and push yourself up. A ladder analogy is the way that novelist Cynthia Eden stays future-focused while she works her way toward her Vision of Success.

"I visualize a ladder in my mind when I think of my writing," she says. "I know that when I started, I was on the bottom rung, just beginning, learning as much as I could about the craft and the industry. Gradually, I've moved up that ladder. I picture myself on that ladder every now and then, and I like the progress I've made. It reaffirms my dedication to my chosen career."

In order to achieve your vision and stay future-focused as an aspiring writer, you have to identify the rungs on your personal ladder that you need to climb in order to reach the top. These are your Vision of Success *Plus* milestones. Then you must act as if you are constantly striving to go one rung higher on the ladder of your writing success.

Passion, Vision, Commitment

Acting as if you are a future-focused writer means keeping what you want at the forefront of your mind at all times, and working every day toward your Vision of Success. It means having passion, vision, and commitment toward your writing goals. It means that when it is time for you to sit down and start writing for the day, you do that, because you know that you are working toward something that you will eventually achieve.

Cultivating a sense of passion, vision, and commitment is what has kept bestselling author CJ Lyons going through the many ups and downs of her now-successful writing career. "The guiding principles that kept me going as I put myself through college and then worked three jobs to get through medical school are the same ones that have motivated my writing. They are vision, know what you want; passion, know why you want it; and commitment, know what you're willing to do to get it."

CJ's comment goes back to the earlier discussion on the topic of *acting as if* you are self-motivated, and the question I always asked myself when I was having a hard time getting out of bed at 3:30 A.M. to write before work—how bad do you want it? When you act as if you want it badly, and you probably do, eventually you will take the steps necessary to achieve success however you define it.

Acting As If You Are Task-Oriented

A huge problem that I hear about in my writing classes is a difficulty remaining task-oriented. Many aspiring authors have no problem setting a writing schedule, getting to their desks, and opening their work-in-progress files. But once there, the writing plan disintegrates because these aspiring authors allow themselves to get distracted by e-mail, the Internet, online shopping, celebrity gossip sites, and social networking sites. Their minds wander. They stare out the window. They wonder what they should have for lunch. They make a grocery list. They have difficulty focusing on the work in front of them. Not exactly the way to get any writing done, is it?

On the other hand, a task-oriented writer sits down, eliminates all distractions, and writes. A task-oriented writer refuses to cave in to writer's freeze, resistance to writing, or procrastination. Let's look at some ways that you can organize yourself to stay focused and act as if you are a task-oriented writer.

Plan Your Work the Day Before

Most successful authors know what they will be working on when they sit down to write. This is one of the benefits of having daily writing goals and keeping a record of your progress toward those goals. For instance, if your goal is to write 1,000 words per day, then you know when you sit down that you need to get 1,000 words on the page. You should also write yourself a note at the end of your daily writing session about where you need to pick up the next time. A trick Ernest Hemingway used was to stop in the middle of a sentence so that he would have a place to start writing the next day. Some writers quickly reread what they wrote the day before as a way to warm up. You need a similar trick to jog your memory about where you are in your work-in-progress.

Daily Direction

Act as if your harsh internal editor is an internal cheerleader instead. Whenever you edit the previous day's work, make notes in the margin with your red pen about what you did right instead of what you did wrong. Give yourself lots of compliments and use your areas of writing strengths as your jumping off point for that day.

Eliminate Distractions

The key to avoid getting pulled down the rabbit hole of not writing is to recognize your distractions and take steps to eliminate or at least control these before you sit down to write. As I have mentioned, this is one of the biggest issues I see in my writing classes with new and aspiring authors. Distractions range from everything to writing around a job to dealing with family members to the mundane distractions of e-mail and Internet. (E-mail and Internet surfing are huge problems for most writers. I recently had a student in one of my classes who told me that she discovered, through my class, that she was spending more than three hours every day checking e-mail and surfing the Net. This was after working at a job all day. She took my class to find out why she never had time to write!)

If the way you avoid writing is to surf the Internet or check e-mail, and so on, close out your browser and your e-mail program as soon as you boot up your computer. Just don't go there. There are applications you can download to block some of these sites for a specified amount of time. Even better, write on a laptop that does not connect to the Internet (which is what I do), or use an AlphaSmart, which is a keyboarding device similar to a laptop that can be used only for word processing functions.

If children or family members in the household are your distraction, talk to them beforehand about needing your time to write. Post your schedule. Tell them what time you will be available to them again that day and then go write. If you have to watch small children, learn to write while they are in the room. Make a commitment to your writing and then find a way to get it done.

At the frantic pace that life moves these days, most writers, even established ones, have very little time to sit down and actually get fresh material on the page. Don't waste your precious hour or two of daily writing time. Act as if you are a task-oriented writer by protecting your writing from distractions.

Act As If You Have a Deadline

In my interviews with successful authors, I have discovered that more than anything else, a deadline is the most effective tool for helping writers write. Most successful authors used this trick even before they were career published in order to stay on track with their writing goals. They set a time frame for finishing their manuscripts and then stuck to that time frame as if there were an agent or editor actually waiting for the submission. This time frame should be a part of your writing goals. In other words, you will write 1,000 words a day, five days a week, for five months in order to complete a 100,000-word novel by a certain date. Then exercise self-discipline in order to meet that self-imposed deadline.

Acting as if you have a deadline before you are published is good practice for staying task-oriented when you are published and there really is an editor waiting for your book by a certain time.

Activity: Now Act As If

Think about a time from your writing life that you wanted to act confident, motivated, task-oriented, or future-focused but failed to do so. Write about this experience in your journal. What was the situation? Who else was involved? What were you thinking and feeling at the time and how did this impact your behavior?

Now write down how you think the scene would had played out if you had acted as if you were confident, motivated, task-oriented, or future focused. What are the main differences in how the situation plays out versus what really happened? Note what your thoughts and feelings were at the time, then note how they are when you mentally act as if. How does *acting as if* affect your thought-feeling-behavior cycle?

Rewrite the scene again, this time making it play out perfectly using the Acting As If technique. Read it aloud. Note how you feel, and what thoughts are connected to these feelings.

Write an Acting As If scene for each trouble spot in your writing life, each time making the scene play out perfectly so that you succeed in the end. Then, the next time you hit that trouble spot, pull out your script and follow it to put Acting As If into practice.

Live Your Life Write

Acting As If is a practical psychological strategy that can positively impact your thought-feeling-behavior cycle in ways that move you toward achieving your writing goals.

- *Acting as if* helps program your subconscious mind to bring about your desired outcome because you are changing your mental constructs, or belief systems, about yourself in positive ways.
- *Acting as if* is a proven technique for overcoming obstacles to personal growth.
- *Acting as if* can help you become more confident in your abilities, motivated to strive toward your goals, task-oriented on a day-to-day basis, and more future-focused.

Chapter 11

Key
Writer Self-Image
Words

So FAR YOU HAVE ESTABLISHED a Vision of Success *Plus* and created milestones to guide your daily choices related to writing as a way of helping you write every day and achieve your vision. You have learned how to identify your thought-feeling-behavior cycle, taken a look at how it is affecting your writing life, and created alternative thoughts, feelings, and behaviors for problematic ones. You have taken responsibility for your writing success through the use of "I" statements and made strides toward improving your Writer Self-Image through role-modeling and Image Incorporation.

Here, we will discuss the idea of key Writer Self-Image words. (Please note that the terms "key Writer Self-Image words" and "key self-image words" are interchangeable.) Key self-image words help you bring the craft of writing into your daily life because they help you focus on writing more frequently, even when you are away from your desk. Dwelling as much as possible on your desired outcome is an effective way to program the subconscious mind to help you achieve that outcome, and using these words is a powerful way to do that. This fun and easy technique is a way to keep your vision in the forefront of your mind at all times, even when you are not writing.

What Are Key Self-Image Words?

Key self-image words are usually single words or two word phrases that you can easily focus on and repeat in your mind as you move through your day. We will discuss the different variations and ways you can use key self-image words to help attain your writing goals. For now, some examples of key self-image words include:

- published author
- bestselling author
- disciplined writer
- finished novel
- daily writer

You can pull these words from your Vision of Success *Plus*; your list of milestones; your list of your role-model's habits and attributes; your positive thoughts, feelings, and behaviors lists; or your list of reasons of why you want to achieve your writing goals. These key words bolster your esteem as a writer and are a one or two word reminder to your subconscious mind about what you are striving to attain.

The Write Stuff

"Developing a writing career

is a marathon, not a sprint."

—Author Annette Fix

Key Self-Image Words Help You Control Your Thoughts

It's important to keep your thoughts on the right track when you are away from your desk. Remember, you have thousands of thoughts every day, and not all of them rise to the level of conscious thinking. This is why you have been working so hard to uncover your inner dialogue and combat the negative thoughts that would keep you from achieving your writing goals.

By using key self-image words, you train your thoughts to stay in alignment with your Vision of Success, because the reality is that you are not able to write constantly and lead a functional life; you have to attend to your family's needs, your job, your health, your social obligations, your pets, and so forth. Even professional writers have to put writing aside each day and tend to other things; no one can (or should) allow herself to be occupied by one activity to the healthy exclusion of a well-rounded life. However, at times when you cannot be actively engaged in working toward your dream, such as when you are at work, tending to household chores, balancing your checkbook, and so on, the usage of key self-image words allows you to continually work on programming your subconscious mind. It's like laying down tracks in a specific direction for your train of thought to follow. And training your thoughts to flow in the direction that you want them to and in a way that will lead you to feel and act in ways that lead to success as a writer is the foundation skill for controlling your thought-feeling-behavior cycle.

The problem for many aspiring writers is that they don't think about writing *enough*. This is an offshoot of a number of psychological dynamics that we have already discussed: avoidance, fear of failure, fear of success, and so forth. Many aspiring writers don't take their writing goals and Vision of Success seriously enough to work their plan over a long period of time, nor do they believe that they have the skill level necessary to achieve it. So they tend to allow themselves to become distracted by the many demands of day to day life and, by default, watch their writing dream wither slowly away.

You do not have to let this happen to you. You can lead a busy life and still shoehorn in daily progress toward your writing goals and Vision of Success. Thinking about writing more and focusing on your goals and Vision of Success will help you shape it into reality.

Daily Direction

When you are suffering from writer's block, sit at your computer and type anything, even if it's nonsense. The goal is to get your fingers moving and the creative flow stimulated. When you feel ready, open your eyes and move to your work-in-progress.

How Do Key Self-Image Words Work?

Key self-image words keep your Vision of Success integrated into your daily routine and speed up the programming process of your subconscious mind. Whenever you focus on something with your conscious mind for a prolonged period, it eventually programs your subconscious mind to help create whatever you are thinking about and manifest it.

I am not talking about thinking about writing as opposed to actually sitting down and writing. You still have to take action. I am talking about the time that you *have* to spend away from writing to tend to your other life obligations—your job, your kids, your marriage, your social obligations. Key self-image words are a way to keep the image of yourself as a writer in the forefront of your mind and steep the idea of writing and becoming a successful writer into every aspect of your life. This way, it becomes an integral part of your thinking patterns and helps bring more and more writing into your daily life.

There is a saying: Don't dress for where you are, dress for where you want to go. In the same way, you need to dress your mind with your Writer Self-Image, and key self-image words help you do this.

Choosing Your Key Writer Self-Image Words

There are a number of different ways that you can create your own Writer Self-Image words and capitalize on their power to achieve your writing dreams. Let's take a look at some of those ways now.

Project into the Future

Just as you looked twenty years into the future to create your Vision of Success *Plus* milestones, you do the same thing when creating your key Writer Self-Image words. Get an image of your Vision of Success in mind—or refer to the milestones you wrote down in your journal—and select two or three words or short phrases that represent your ultimate dream.

One writer who has used this projection technique is Steve Berry, *New York Times* bestselling author of *The Paris Vendetta* and other novels, who aspired to get published by a New York house. He held on to that image over the course of twelve years and through eighty-five rejection letters. Berry kept his thoughts honed on that image of himself as an author published by a New York house as a way of navigating the milestones of his Vision of Success. His key self-image words during that time might have been "New York publisher" or "New York author."

Whatever word or short phrase represents your writing dream is a good choice for a Writer Self-Image key word—a popular key self-image phrase that may nicely encapsulate your dream is "bestselling author." The only requirement is that this word or phrase is meaningful to you. This is a subjective experience. To check your key self-image word's power, repeat it out loud and see if it resonates with you. If it does, then it is effective enough to influence your subconscious mind.

Achieve One-, Three-, and Five-Year Milestones

A good use of this technique is to use key self-image words to accomplish your one-, three-, and five-year milestones. Key self-image words keep your short-term vision honed in on what your behaviors and actions should be in order to achieve those earlier milestones. For example, if your goal at this point is to simply finish your novel, your key words might be "finish," "finished novel," and so on. If you are actively looking for an agent and want to attract someone who is a good match for you, you might choose simply "agent" or "matching agent" or "good agent."

If you are trying to break into the magazine market as a freelancer, you may use "freelancer" as your key word. If you are trying to sell your first novel, try "novelist." If a writing award is your goal, you might use "award-winning author." Combinations of key words such as "successful author," "published author," "published novelist," and so forth make good key self-image words. Remember, any word or short two word phrase that encapsulates or helps you get to your overall goal is what you are trying to distill into your key self-image words.

Short-Term Writing Success

You can also use key Writer Self-Image words to achieve your short-term writing milestones, or those that you want to accomplish within six months or less. This area is where many new writers get tripped up; they know where they want to go—become a published novelist—but they don't know exactly how to get there.

Many hopeful newbies start out strong by writing for a few days or weeks, but then their motivation and enthusiasm taper off. They stop writing, and writing becomes once again only a wish instead of a dream that they are activity pursuing. If you are a new writer, don't fall into this trap. Use key self-image words that help you stay on track and avoid this pitfall.

The Write Stuff

"If I'm 'blocked' there always ends up being a good reason for it. So I relax and go with the flow, then just catch up once I figure out the problem and get back on track."

—Bestselling author CJ Lyons

There are a variety of ways to do this. Go back to your ideal Writer Self-Image. What traits, attributes, and values does that writer possess? Pull key self-image words from that list. For instance, if you are having trouble sitting down to write on a consistent basis, your ideal Writer Self-Image for now needs to be of someone who writes every day, or at least four or five days out of the week. In this case, your key self-image word might simply be "write." Or it might be your daily word count goal, such as "1,200 words."

I have some friends who are practicing to run a marathon. They use the phrase "26.2," or the number of miles in a marathon, as a mantra throughout the day to remind them of their goal. They frequently say to themselves, "26.2, 26.2." It keeps their enthusiasm high and their commitment solid. In a similar way, you can use your word count goal as a powerful reminder of what you are striving for each day.

If you are attempting a new writing schedule, you can use the name of that schedule as your key image phrase; for instance, someone trying to establish a before-work writing schedule might use "early morning writer" as their key image phrase. Any word or two-word phrase that stamps the image of you working a schedule on your subconscious mind will work.

Again, I like what I call "finishing" goals because they have urgency and immediacy to them that creates energy to complete them. So, the word "finish" is a useful key self-image word. If you need to complete an essay by a certain date in order to submit it to an anthology, use the phrase "finish essay." If you are struggling to complete the novel you've been trying to write for three years, try "finish novel." If you need to get a query and a synopsis completed so you can search for a publisher, use the key self-image words "finish synopsis" or something similar.

Improve Writer Confidence

Key Writer Self-Image words are a great way to boost your confidence levels as a writer. If you have completed a manuscript and want to successfully query an agent, "successful query" might be appropriate in that case. If you want to ensure that you come across as confident in yourself in the letter, use the key words "confident" or "confidence." To bolster flagging motivation to complete a work-in-progress, try "successful author" or "published author." You should use anything that will remind you of what you are working toward and create feelings of positive well-being within yourself.

Focus On Your Why

Key writer self-image words help you focus on the *why* of why you want to become a successful author. In turn, this generates motivation, enthusiasm, and dedication for working on your long-term writing goals.

This strategy is one that many successful authors use to stay focused on their dream and to overcome any self-doubt. Annette Fix, author of *The Break-Up Diet*, says that, for her, focusing on key components of what success means to her boosts her confidence levels and her belief in her abilities as a writer. "Success to me is doing something I love and getting paid for it," she says. "Not many people can say their career and their passion are one and the same."

You can do the same. Choose key Writer Self-Image words culled from the list of reasons why you want to become a successful author to inspire you to persevere toward your dream.

Memorize Key Words

You can also choose two or three of the more important key self-image words, perhaps one that represents your Vision of Success and one that targets a specific problem area you want to address for a few weeks, and memorize them. Then, whenever you are driving, at work, shopping, watching television, sitting in meetings, doing household chores, or in general just going about your daily activities, let the key Writer Self-Image word or phrase act as a mantra; simply repeat it mentally, over and over. Doing this will imprint the image of that goal on to your subconscious mind.

Daily Direction

Use your key Writer Self-Image words throughout the day by silently repeating them to yourself at every opportunity. This speeds up the subconscious mind programming process and builds your Writer Self-Image.

The Importance of Enthusiasm

Whenever you speak or think key self-image words or phrases, it is important to actually feel how you will really feel when you achieve the goal that the key word or phrase represents. Emotion in the form of enthusiasm fuels your subconscious mind and helps speed up the programming process that makes your goals and dreams manifest into reality. Whether you are driving in your car, sitting in a meeting at work, waiting to pick up your child from school, or eating your lunch, infuse your key Writer Self-Image words and phrases with the positive, uplifting emotions that you will actually feel when the goal is realized. In this way, key self-image words and phrases become a very powerful way to stamp your subconscious mind and keep your thoughts tracking toward your writing goals whenever you are away from your desk.

Activity: Identifying Your Key Writer Self-Image Words

Go back in your journal notes and pick out five to ten key Writer Self-Image words and record them in a separate section of your notebook. Transfer these words to index cards. Keep these cards in your purse or briefcase and scroll through them at every opportunity. You might write your chosen words on a couple of cards and place them in places you will see them frequently, like the dashboard of your car, the bathroom mirror, above your computer monitor, beside your alarm clock, and so forth.

I have included some key self-image word lists below for you to use as examples. Feel free to use these if they resonate with you, or create your own. Your specific key words will depend on where you are in your writing career and what particular challenges to achieving your writing dream that you currently face.

Examples of key Writer Self-Image words to achieve a Vision of Success:

- Bestselling author
- Thriller/Romance/Sci-Fi author
- Working author
- New York house

- Successful author
- Published author

Examples of key Writer Self-Image words from a short-term Vision of Success *Plus* Milestone:

- Write
- Write daily
- Write novel
- After-hours writer
- Book contract
- Finish trilogy

Examples of key Writer Self-Image Words Pulled from Reasons for Accomplishing Goal:

- Legacy
- Accomplish
- Achieve dream
- Publish
- Family legacy

Examples of key Writer Self-Image words to Instill Confidence and Belief in Your Abilities:

- Confidence
- Confident
- Persistent
- Worthy
- Capable

Feel free to use these key self-image words or to create your own list. The only necessary qualification is that the words are meaningful to you and resonate with you.

Live Your Life Write

Key Writer Self-Image words are powerful images of your dream that keep your thoughts tracking in a positive direction. Dwelling on key self-image words when you are away from your writing helps stamp your ideal Writer Self-Image onto your subconscious mind and speeds up the programming process. Remember:

- You can use multiple key Writer Self-Image words at a time for as long as it takes to create your Vision of Success.
- Cull your list from your Vision of Success *Plus*, your milestones, the reasons why you want to accomplish your writing goals, and problem areas such as lack of confidence in your abilities.
- Write your words on index cards and post them in places you will see it often. Memorize them and repeat them often, either out loud or silently.
- Key image words help you control your thoughts and feelings and impact your behavior in ways that keep you working toward your writing dream.

Chapter 12

Your Writer

Self-Image

Script

ANOTHER RESOURCE YOU CAN USE when dealing with your thought-feeling-behavior cycle and learning to direct it toward success as a writer is called *scripts* in psychology. In the simplest of terms, scripts are a series of statements that you tell yourself in any given situation that guide your behavior. For the purposes of this book, we will be focusing exclusively on scripts as they are related to writing and your daily writing habits.

Here, we will discuss scripts, how they relate to your Writer Self-Image, and how your script is affecting your efforts to attain both long-term and daily writing success. You will learn how to identify your writer self-image script and make changes to it so that it becomes a tool in your writer toolbox that helps you write every day and helps maintain your enthusiasm, motivation, and dedication to your long-term writing goals.

How Scripts Work

Remember that, on a subconscious level, you have an ongoing inner dialogue that creates your feelings and thoughts, which subsequently drive your behavior. This inner dialogue is essentially what makes up your scripts. Any time you are presented with a situation, either one that is known to you or one that is new, you rely on your script to help you know how to act. People create scripts based on past experiences and their own mental beliefs about themselves and their abilities.

Again, scripts are a series of statements that you tell yourself in certain situations that guide your behaviors. It's a way that your mind helps you organize information and get through the day effectively. A script helps you navigate through life without having to stop and figure out how to do something each and every time.

The Write Stuff

"To avoid crashing, a writer has to maintain enthusiasm the way an aircraft has to maintain altitude."

—Novelist Alan Bradley

Here is a simple example. Let's say you are going out to eat at a restaurant. Because you have eaten at restaurants many times over your life, you have developed certain scripts that help you know what to do. You know that you wait to be seated, you place your order with a server, you wait for your meal to be delivered, you eat, you pay your bill, and you leave a tip on the table. No matter what restaurant you go to, those are the basic steps to eating there. When you walk into a restaurant that you've never been in before, your mind helps you know what to do based on your past experiences with other restaurants. Even if you are particularly hungry, you still follow those steps. You don't walk in, charge straight into the kitchen, and take something from the refrigerator. You follow the steps that your inner script dictates.

When it comes to writing, your scripts define behaviors that over time become habits that fit your self-fulfilling prophecy and program your subconscious mind to bring about certain outcomes.

Your script manifests itself in all situations related to your writing: from day-to-day work habits to your plans for sending out work to how you present yourself at conferences or other opportunities where you might run into agents and editors. The nice thing is that you can change your writing script if you don't like it.

Scripts in Action

If you go back to the "I" statement exercise from Chapter 5, you can determine your own Writer Self-Image script by looking at the trouble spots where you needed to develop "I" statements. For instance, in the example I gave, the thoughts *I have submitted my manuscript to twenty agents and none of them have taken it. Something is wrong with my writing* are followed by *I must not be a very good writer or have very good ideas since no one has accepted me as a client.*

If a writer indulges in these types of thoughts and feelings, over time a script is written. This script includes erroneous perceptions that the writer isn't good because he doesn't yet have an agent, that something is wrong with his writing, and so forth.

It is not difficult to see how this script leads to more feelings of discouragement. The behaviors that would result are most likely giving up, self-sabotaging, and so on.

Repetition Is Key

With enough repetition a script (either negative or positive) becomes the guiding force in a writer's life. Research demonstrates that persistent thoughts and feelings actually wear grooves into your brain that become a rigid pattern that your conscious mind follows, like a train on tracks. The result is that the same thought-feeling-behavior cycle is played out repeatedly. With each repetition the groove gets deeper, the thought-feeling-behavior cycle gets more entrenched, and then your subconscious mind programming kicks in. Eventually your script starts to predetermine your behavior. But you can change the groove of your track by examining your Writer Self-Image script.

You Want Your Script to Shout Success

Going again to our example from Chapter 5, you can see how the script in that situation is likely shaping up: *I have submitted my manuscript to twenty agents and none of them have taken it. Something is wrong with my writing. I must not be a very good writer or have very good ideas since no one has accepted me as a client.*

What other thoughts might follow? Probably thoughts along the lines of: *Why do I bother to keep trying? I'm wasting my time. This takes too long and it's too much work. I'll never succeed.* All of these thoughts are accompanied by feelings of despair and discouragement. Because a script over time predetermines actions, the writer in this situation would begin to have these feelings prior to ever sitting down at her desk, prior to ever having these thoughts, at least at a conscious level.

You want your script to scream success and to reflect an author who has confidence, enthusiasm, motivation, and dedication. You want your script to bolster you on those days when the writing is hard, or when you just received your fifteenth rejection letter for your novel, or when you are at some particular low point in your career. Your script, what you tell yourself during these times, will give you the fortitude to press on.

A writer whose script bolstered her belief in herself and her writing abilities would create positive feelings of anticipation about writing. This writer looks forward to the day's work. She works a schedule. Her mental beliefs in herself as a writer promote encouraging feelings about her future as a writer. Her actions every day increase her chances of becoming a successful author. She writes, submits work, exudes confidence, doesn't allow rejection to sway her from her goals, and so forth.

The Write Stuff

"Writer's block is simply perfectionism with a scary name."

—Author Amber Leigh Williams

Define Your Script's Theme

For our purposes here, scripts can be categorized according to theme. Identifying your scripts theme will help you take steps to correct it to a more positive one. Some of these scripts themes include:

- Poor Me Script: This type of script can be very debilitating to writers. The general theme of this script is *Nobody is ever going to publish anything I write.*
- Odd Man Out Script: The general theme of this script is *I'm not good enough to get published,* as if publishing were some sort of elite club to which you cannot gain admission.

Some additional scripts include the following.

Favoritism Script

Scripts that are of what I call a "favoritism" slant tend to make you think that successful writers got some kind of lucky break that you are not going to get, such as a lucrative contact in the field, being in the right place at the right time, or that they had some already successful mentor who helped them achieve their success. These scripts contain thoughts like *Authors who make it got a lucky break. They got lucky.*

"Yes...But" Script

A common script is the one that allows you have a limited amount of success but puts restrictions on what you can actually attain. This script is for someone who has perhaps achieved a small amount of writing success—perhaps had some articles published in local papers—but who craves wider success and believes that they cannot achieve it. I call this the "Yes...but" script: *Yes, I got published once, but that's probably as far as I'll go.*

These categories of scripts cause damage to your chances of success because, for obvious reasons, they deflate your enthusiasm and drive to succeed before you ever get around to picking up a pen and paper. They demoralize you in advance and prevent you from sitting down at your desk and banging out your manuscript. These scripts simply stop you cold in your tracks. Happily, you can change a negative script into a positive one, which we'll discuss in just a minute.

Successful Writers' Negative Scripts

Every writer, even successful ones, have scripts, both good and bad. Negative scripts are where self-doubt, writer's block, and resistance to writing spring. All writers have them, throughout their entire careers. The key is to pin yours down and actively work to change it.

"You always wonder if you're good enough or could be better," says novelist Debra Webb. "I once had a *New York Times* bestselling author, one who had made that prestigious list many times over, say to me that she wasn't sure she had a 'great' book in her. So, even she doubted that what she had done to date was what she would like it to be."

Negative scripts can cause successful writers to have writer's block in the form of the fear of success that we discussed earlier. Novelist Amber Leigh Williams says, "I fear a blank page but I fear more filling it with something that doesn't work."

Even though successful writers still struggle with negative scripts in the form of doubt and writer's block, what makes them successful is that they have changed their thought-feeling-behavior cycle in ways that allow them to keep writing.

Identify Behavioral Manifestations

After you have identified your script and its theme, the next step is to identify what types of behaviors your script is manifesting. Do you avoid writing? Do you set a writing schedule but then consistently fail to meet it? Do you harshly judge your work and not allow yourself the flexibility to make mistakes and grow as a writer? There are many ways that a negative script can manifest in your writing life:

- **Comparison:** This occurs when you compare where you are on your path with another, probably more successful writer. You end up feeling jealous, discouraged, and maybe even angry. While using another writer as a role-model to help you achieve your own dreams is a healthy tool as we discussed in Chapter 8, comparing yourself to another writer in ways that leave you holding the short end of the stick is not healthy.
- **Avoiding writing:** A negative script will sap your enthusiasm and motivation to write.
- **Giving up easily:** A negative script does not supply you with the confidence in yourself to keep going through rejection.
- **Judging your work too harshly:** You are unable to pick out the good elements of your writing and build upon those.

Over time, all of these factors will lead to not writing, and becoming a writer will remain a wish instead of a dream that is actively pursued.

Changing Your Script

The way to change a negative script and its theme is to rewrite the script and define the new behaviors that you want to see happen. Using the same example, here is the old script rewritten into something more positive, goal-directed, and future-focused:

Old Script: *I have submitted my manuscript to twenty agents, and none of them have taken it. Something is wrong with my writing. I must not be a very good writer or have very good ideas since no one has accepted me as a client. Why do I bother to keep trying? I'm wasting my time. This takes too long and it's too much work. I'll never succeed.*

New Script: *I have submitted my manuscript to twenty agents and, so far, none of them have taken it. I am still learning the craft of writing, and while no one has accepted me as a client yet, if I keep trying I will succeed. Learning any new skill takes time. My dream of becoming a successful writer is a lot of work, but it's worth it, because soon I will succeed.*

Read the two scripts out loud and notice how you feel. While the first one is demoralizing, the second one charges you up and makes you eager to get to your desk. While script one's theme is "poor me," the second script's theme is "I can do it!" You feel excited about your future as a writer. You believe you can get there. You feel enthusiastic, motivated, and dedicated to your journey of becoming a successful author. Which writer would you rather be?

Define New Behaviors of a New Script

The final element to changing a script is to define the new behaviors that you want to see with the positive script and theme. Examples of goal-directed behaviors that spring from a positive script including getting to your desk every day to write, saying encouraging things to yourself when you get stuck or write something that is not as good as you would like it to be, and feeling good about your efforts to find success as an author.

Changing your writing script is a useful strategy for finding ways to pump up your enthusiasm, motivation, and dedication to your writing dream. Looking at your script and ensuring that it is positive, future-focused, and inspires action is a key way that you can recharge yourself and get to your desk over and over again, writing.

Activity: Improving Your Writer Self-Image Script

Sit for about twenty minutes in a quiet area, such as a park, in a quiet room of your house, or in the library. Take a few minutes to get totally relaxed. Then think of a situation where you believe you may been influenced by a negative script. This might have been the time that you allowed a rejection letter to prevent you from writing for two weeks. Maybe you have not been as disciplined with your writing schedule as you need to be in order to achieve your goals. You can also solicit help from your subconscious mind. Ask: Subconscious, is my Writer Self-Image script interfering with my success? Let thoughts and images arise without censoring them.

Next, observe yourself in your mind going through the actions of the situation. Ask your subconscious mind to offer up the various statements you were making to yourself on a deep level during this situation that might define a script. Try to get at least three or four statements, then notice the corresponding feelings those statements create within you.

Write your script statements, your feelings, and any other insights that came to you during the meditation down in your journal.

Write a New Script

Next, in your journal change every negative statement of your script into a positive one. Read these new statements out loud and notice how you feel. Write those feelings down. List at least two ways that you want these new positive thoughts and feelings to manifest behaviorally in your writing life. If you choose, post your new script on an index card near your computer so that you can see it every time you sit down to write.

Live Your Life Write

Scripts are thoughts grouped together in a pattern that you tell yourself about yourself and your writing abilities. Scripts determine your actions in advance of writing for the day, and they are integral to the formation and ongoing shaping of your Writer Self-Image. Key points to remember about your Writer Self-Image Script include the following:

- A script becomes the guiding force in a writer's life, whether it is positive or negative.
- Successful authors have positive scripts. Their scripts actively determine their daily actions and help them achieve their short- and long-term writing goals by driving their behavior in goal-oriented ways.
- You can change a negative script to a positive one through the use of "I" statements and by taking responsibility for achieving your writing goals. Spend time every day focusing on your intentions, and believe that you can achieve your Vision of Success.

Chapter 13

Positive
Self-*Talk*

NOW THAT YOU HAVE WORKED TO RECOGNIZE these thoughts that so often dictate your feelings and behaviors, sometimes without your conscious realization, and you have identified a script, pinpointed problem areas, and changed negative thoughts for better, more success-oriented ones, it's time to discuss the importance of Positive Self-Talk. Self-talk is just that: the things that you say to yourself—both out loud and silently—that either enhance or hinder your chances of success. In this chapter, you will learn how to create positive self-talk statements that will bring the craft of writing into your daily life and help you achieve your long-term writing success.

The Importance of Optimism in Success

Cultivating an optimistic outlook toward your life as a writer is an important part of bringing writing into your daily life and achieving success, however you define it. Psychological research has demonstrated that people who attribute events in their lives to causes that are permanent and that they have little to no control over tend to become depressed. They lean toward pessimism in their day to day lives and interpret the majority of events in their lives in a negative way. You can see how this creates a negative thought-feeling-behavior cycle. If you constantly believe that what happens to you is because of unchangeable circumstances beyond any of your control, you feel powerless; you probably will not act in ways that enhance your chances of succeeding. Pessimism sets up a negative self-fulfilling prophecy. Eventually, people with this mind-set begin to feel so utterly powerless to achieve success that they stop trying—a phenomenon known as *learned helplessness*.

On the other hand, people who interpret the events in their lives as springing from temporary circumstances and internal causes—meaning causes that are likely to change and which they can likely influence—tend to feel more in charge of their lives and interpret events in a decidedly more positive way. They view setbacks as temporary failures and they go about figuring out how to overcome that failure. They more easily recover from these setbacks. Their thoughts, feelings, and behaviors reflect a sense of optimism; they believe that no matter what has happened, things will get better for them and they start figuring out how to make that happen.

The Write Stuff

"I've stayed dedicated to my writing because I've never had a Plan B—a back-up career—as a default option for my life. I knew if I created that safety net, I would be too tempted to give up writing and do something easier than giving birth to every word I put onto the page."

—Author Annette Fix

This is where positive self-talk comes in. Optimistic people say and think thoughts that are uplifting and encouraging. They subscribe to a positive self-fulfilling prophecy that allows them to move around obstacles and keep forging ahead with their goals. People who achieve success in any area of life are typically those who have a sunny outlook. My research into the characteristics of successful authors bears this out.

Let me give you an example of how this works. Think about a time when a piece of your writing was rejected. What thoughts went through your head? Did you believe that your writing was rejected because you are a bad writer, or did you believe that the negative reaction was just one editor's opinion? What about when that piece of writing was rejected for the tenth time? The twentieth? What types of thoughts did you have then?

The pessimistic writer is likely to think that editors everywhere will dislike their writing and that that fact will never change. But, on the other hand, an optimistic writer views rejection as having a temporary cause that they can influence—they think that this one editor did not like their writing, that the quality of the writing is within their control, that they can work to improve it, and that eventually they will find an editor who will accept their work.

If this is a trouble spot for you, don't worry. I will give you tools in this chapter to start changing your outlook to an optimistic one designed to achieve results.

Internal Locus of Control

Do you see the difference in the two lines of thinking in the above example? Whereas the pessimistic writer views rejection as something that is likely to be permanent and nothing she can do will change that, the optimistic writer takes responsibility for the rejection by mentally reframing it: she chalks it up to just this one editor instead of generalizing to all editors everywhere, and she starts her thoughts down the track of thinking that she can continue to improve the quality of her writing until she finally gets an acceptance.

Consider the impact of these two lines of viewing rejection. Which writer is likely to continue writing every day? The optimistic writer gets my vote.

The optimistic writer has what, in psychology, is called an *internal locus of control*. People with an internal locus of control believe that they are largely in charge of what happens to them in life, and that what they do makes a difference in the various outcomes they are seeking. People with an external locus of control believe that they have little to no power over what happens in their lives and that events happen to them randomly. While no one can control everything that happens to them at all times, how you view situations impacts your thought-feeling-behavior cycle. The interesting part about an internal/external locus of control is that whichever way you believe makes it so; your locus of control creates your self-fulfilling prophecy.

Daily Direction

To bring more writing into your daily life, look at your schedule hour by hour and pinpoint one task that you can eliminate, delegate, or cut back on by twenty minutes. Then use those twenty minutes for writing, instead.

It's important to have an optimistic attitude and to cultivate an internal locus of control. All of this links back to the work you did in Chapter 5 on "I" statements. Taking responsibility for the events that happen to you in your writing life creates an empowering mind-set and keeps your attitude toward your writing optimistic. This influences your thought-feeling-behavior-cycle to stay moving in a goal-directed manner. The writer who is optimistic toward writing will write every day, view rejection as a challenge to improve, take calculated risks that enhance chances of success, and believe that eventually, if she keeps at it, she will succeed as a writer however she defines it.

Optimism and positive self-talk play huge roles in successful writers' lives. The cornerstone of their mind-set is the attitude that they will achieve no matter what. This is not to say that successful authors don't have bad days, because everyone does. But the key to continuing to move forward with your goals is how you interpret the event that has set you back and how you plan—or don't plan—to overcome it. In most cases, shifting from a pessimistic to an optimistic outlook is simply a matter of changing how you interpret the events in your life. Positive self-talk is the way to do this.

Uses of Positive Self-Talk for Writers

There are a number of ways that you can use positive self-talk to help you achieve your daily and long-term writing goals. To shift your mind-set, use positive self-talk by asking questions of yourself that will get your thoughts flowing in a new, positive direction and reframe a situation or how you're feeling about a situation. Think of positive self-talk as a way to talk to yourself as if you were talking to a dear friend to whom you want to provide encouragement and direction. Let's take a look at some specific examples.

Am I Doing What I Want to Do?

"Am I doing what I want to do?" This is a powerful question that cuts to the heart of the matter. It focuses your mind on what is important right here, right now. If you want to finish your novel, sleeping late every morning or watching reruns every night is not going to accomplish that goal. When you ask yourself "Am I doing what I want to do?" you can quickly determine if your current activity enhances or hinders your chances of writing success.

The Write Stuff

"When I had a setback, I went back to the page. That's still what I do when I'm discouraged by external factors: I go back to writing my books. My books, which no one else can write."

—Novelist Barbara O'Neal

Successful authors use this type of positive self-talk question to maintain their day-to-day focus on what's important—writing. No matter where you are in terms of publication, daily writing and focusing on the task at hand is the linchpin for success. *New York Times* bestselling author Dianna Love explains how she uses self-talk. "I'm a very disciplined person to begin with when it comes to getting any task done, but I can tell you the longer you're published the more that piles on your plate," she says. "This means even someone with good work habits may have to shift gears often to adjust to the unexpected change in work load when revisions and copy edits show up in the last two weeks of the next book due, and on top of promoting an upcoming release."

Love goes on to explain how she uses positive self-talk to keep her mind focused on the next right step in terms of meeting her daily writing goals. "It gets pretty overwhelming," she says, "but when that happens you just ask yourself, 'Am I doing what I want to do?' If the answer is resounding 'yes,' then you can deal with being overwhelmed and push harder to be productive."

The next time you find yourself watching a soap opera or vacuuming out your car instead of adhering to your writing schedule, ask yourself, "Am I doing what I want to do?" The answer is that you probably want to be working toward your Vision of Success instead. Positive self-talk will help you shift gears and get focused on what's important in that moment—working to achieve those milestones you created for your Vision of Success *Plus*. Those milestones should still be posted prominently where you will see them every day, and every day you should take some action toward achieving them.

Any type of question that focuses on whether or not your current activity is helping you achieve writing success is useful for focusing your efforts. Some examples of positive self-talk to help you stay focused on daily writing goals include:

- Am I doing what I want to do right now?
- Is what I am doing right now helping or hindering my writing goals?
- Writers write. What do I need to do to complete my daily writing goal now?
- How will this help me reach my Vision of Success *Plus* milestones?

Dealing with Rejection

Again, the difference between optimism and pessimism is often in our subtle interpretation of events. Positive self-talk is the key to dealing with failure in any area, and it's critical when you are coping with the level of rejection that all writers must face. When successful authors get a rejection letter, they use it to fuel their determination to improve their craft. They look at rejection through the lens of an internal locus of control; they ask themselves, what can I do to improve? What can I do to get that one yes?

Novelist Lori Foster adopted this mind-set over the ten manuscripts and five years that it took her to get published. "With every rejection letter that I got, and I got plenty, I was more determined to prove myself," she says.

That is the kind of optimistic attitude you should adopt, too. Instead of giving up when you get a rejection letter, say to yourself that you will use the opportunity to improve your craft. You should ask yourself the hard questions—have you really been putting as much work into succeeding as a writer as you know you should? Have you been holding up your end of your Vision of Success *Plus*? Will you actually be able to achieve your milestones on time or have you been slacking off?

Use these examples of positive self-talk to deal with rejection:

- I am getting better with each manuscript I write.
- Eventually I will find an editor who loves my work.
- Every rejection takes me one step closer to that yes.
- If I keep writing, I will eventually be successful.

And remember, rejection is an opportunity to work harder and write more. If you have been writing two hours per week, write three. If you have been writing three hours, write four. Shift your mind-set from pessimistic to optimistic when it comes to rejection.

Chart Successful Writing Careers

Positive self-talk is instrumental in helping successful authors chart their careers. Most successful authors are well-versed in the business side of their careers and adapt their writing styles according to what will bring them the most success at any given point in their career arcs. For instance, many authors bring to their craft a very deliberate approach of learning to write the types of books that have a better chance of selling. This reflects a strong internal locus of control; if you believe you can write what has a better of chance of selling, you will naturally feel motivated to write every day in order to get that potential bestselling manuscript out the door. Some examples of positive self-talk that will help you chart your writing career include:

- I have the ability to learn to write what is selling.
- I can write what sells and also what I enjoy writing.
- What can I do today that will support my writing career?

Novelist Nancy Martin gives an example of how she did it. "Years ago, I deliberately set out to make a living as a writer," she says. "To get started, I looked at the business side of things very carefully, and I continue to monitor the industry. I write what sells, as long as I enjoy the writing. And every three years, I re-evaluate where I am, where I want to be, what my financial needs are."

Martin's attitude reflects a positive, optimistic outlook. She adapts what she writes to what is selling. However, notice that she still only writes what she enjoys writing. That's the nice thing about taking responsibility for your writing; you can focus on success yet still enjoy your craft.

Daily Direction

Set your alarm clock five minutes earlier each day for one week. At the end of seven days, you will be getting up thirty-five minutes earlier and can use that time for writing.

Be Your Own Cheerleader

Positive self-talk is a key component of every successful author's day. There is simply no way to keep writing, day in and day out, over the many years it takes to achieve success without being your own cheerleader. Creative people have a tendency to be very critical of themselves. If this is a problem for you, shifting your mind-set will help you maintain your dedication to your craft. Criticism does not lead to optimism. You have to be on your own side when it comes to writing, and using positive self-talk can help you accomplish this. Many years ago, I put the statement "You Can Do It!" in a small decorative frame near my computer. Anytime I became discouraged, I would look at that statement. It helped, and I still have it to this day.

Other examples of positive self-talk that you can use to encourage yourself include:

- I will succeed.
- I will become a successful writer.
- I am confident in my abilities as an author.
- I believe in myself.

New York Times bestselling author Brenda Novak has said that, in the beginning of her writing career, she felt it was extremely important to believe in herself; she had the mind-set that if she didn't believe in herself, she couldn't really expect any agents or editors or publishers to believe in her, either.

This is the kind of attitude you should adopt, too.

Reinforce Your Strengths

Positive reinforcement is very important when it comes to building optimism. You want to highlight and reward yourself for all the ways you are making progress toward your writing goals. To do this, look at the places where you've had success in your day to day writing life and create a list of positive self-talk statements to reinforce areas in writing where you excel. Some examples include:

- I excel at fulfilling my daily writing schedule.
- I completed a writing task that had previously intimidated me.
- I work every day toward my writing Vision of Success.

Even if it is simply finishing your novel, finally mustering the courage to send out a query to a national magazine, or writing for thirty minutes today, give yourself praise. This will build esteem for your Writer Self-Image.

Activity: Create Positive Self-Talk for Different Writing Scenarios

Now it's time for you to create your own positive self-talk. Using the statements I gave you throughout this chapter as a starting point, create a list of optimistic, uplifting statements you can say to yourself on a regular basis that will motivate you to write every day and keep you focused on achieving your milestones. Pay particular attention to trouble areas that you consistently experience. For example, if daily writing is a challenge for you, make a list of positive self-talk statements that you will say to yourself to get to your desk every day. If finishing projects is a trouble spot, make a list of statements for that area as well.

Remember to also make a list of statements for areas that you excel in. Cheering yourself on in this manner will keep your inspiration levels high, and motivate you in the face of discouragement.

Refer back to the mirror activities that you did in Chapter 7 and use your positive self- talk statements in a similar manner. Repetition of your statements helps to program the subconscious mind to create your desired results.

Live Your Life Write

Positive self-talk is an important piece of building optimism toward writing, bringing the craft of writing into your daily life, and achieving your desired writing results. Positive self-talk statements are things that you say to yourself, both mentally and externally, that either enhance or hinder your chances of success. Optimism and positive self-talk play huge roles in successful writers' lives. The attitude that they will achieve no matter what is usually the cornerstone of their mind-set. Remember:

- Develop an internal locus of control by interpreting the events in your writing life as having an internal, temporary cause, meaning something that you can influence through your actions; this helps you feel more empowered to achieve the outcomes you seek in your writing life.
- Successful authors are optimistic authors. Strive to build optimism in your daily writing life through the use of positive self-talk.
- Create positive self-talk statements for every trouble spot in your writing life as well as the areas you excel. Positive reinforcement of strengths is a key factor in building high esteem in your Writer Self-Image.

part iii

Deepen Your Writing

In this part, we will discuss how you can deepen your writing practice as you work to bring more of the craft of writing into your daily life. When you deepen your writing process, you enhance your Writer Self-Image. Writing becomes a natural part of your daily life. You don't simply write, you become a writer. And when you become a writer, you are naturally inclined to weave writing into your daily routine. As you begin to write more, you construct a bridge from your conscious to your subconscious mind and learn how to tap into your bottomless well of creativity. Writing becomes a natural part of your life, and is as essential as breathing.

Chapter 14

Your *Writing* Counselors

WRITING COUNSELORS SPRING FROM YOUR SUBCONSCIOUS MIND, and they are a manifestation of your subconscious wisdom. In this chapter, we will discuss how you can use Writing Counselors to capitalize on the inherent wisdom and guidance residing in your subconscious mind. This technique is a way of reaching into your vast subconscious and using the resources there to help guide you toward success. It's like having your very own staff of writing advisors on stand-by, twenty-four hours a day!

Creating counselors for various areas of life where success is desired is a concept first introduced by Napoleon Hill. For our purposes, we will look at the various ways that you can create your own writing counselors to help you with writing, anything from bringing writing into your daily life to receiving needed career guidance.

Successful People Use Counselors

The process of obtaining advice and guidance from the subconscious mind through the mechanism of creating counselors, or guides as Napoleon Hill called them, is a technique that many successful people have used. Alexander Graham Bell, Henry Ford, Thomas Edison, and Abraham Lincoln were all known to have relied on some type of subconscious wisdom via counselors or guides to attain needed guidance and advice for their inventions or missions.

Creating writing counselors is a way for you to access your subconscious mind by giving it a form recognizable to your conscious mind. Basically, you create a form—in this case a counselor—that your conscious mind is familiar with, and you then use that form as a mechanism to communicate easily with your subconscious. This gives your subconscious mind a way to funnel information to your conscious mind in an easy to use fashion.

For instance, let's say that you want to ask your subconscious mind what the next scene is in your novel. When you have a recognizable template in the form of a counselor for your conscious mind to imagine, the process of getting the answer from your subconscious happens more quickly. Using an imaginary counselor to get information and guidance from your subconscious mind facilitates and speeds up the mechanism of subconscious communication.

Creating a Counselor

This technique is fun and easy to use; your counselor can take any shape and form that you wish. It can be male, female, an animal, a symbol, an avatar, or even your favorite author role-model. Whatever symbolism resonates with you as someone who can offer support, encouragement, and guidance for your writing will work as your imaginary writing counselor.

There are many uses for writing counselors and many different ways that you can employ this technique in your daily writing life. You can have as many counselors as you want, in as many different categories as you want. Below are some categories you might wish to create.

Daily Writing Counselor

If you are struggling to find time to write in your day to day life, create a writing counselor who will offer you support and encouragement to sit down and write every day. The responsibility of this guide is to help you bring the craft of writing into your daily life by showing you various ways that you can fit writing into your schedule and to show you how to overcome any obstacles that stand in your way. The image of this counselor might be your favorite author or a kindly teacher you had in grade school. It might be a famous historical writer you admire. Or you can create a totally new person to act as your daily writing counselor. This counselor will be the person you turn to, in your mind, for help when you need advice regarding your daily writing habits.

Plot Counselor

If you are struggling with the plot of your novel, seek some guidance from your subconscious mind on what direction to take with your story. Use a plot counselor to discuss your sticking points and to kick around ideas. The responsibility of the plot counselor is to aid you in coming up with plot material. As with the daily writing counselor, the image of this counselor might be that of your favorite author, or a famous author from the past.

Career Guidance Counselor

Career guidance is something that every writer needs—at every stage of his career. It is the sole responsibility of the career counselor to give you sound advice on your writing career. This is a useful guide to use when creating your Vision of Success *Plus* milestones. A career guidance counselor is one who will provide you with the subconscious mind's wisdom regarding every aspect of your writing career.

Idea Counselor

An idea counselor's charge is to help you generate fresh ideas for stories, articles, essays, and poems. Your idea counselor can offer up new angles on old ideas to help make them more marketable. When you are stuck for ideas, an idea counselor will help you get your creative process flowing again.

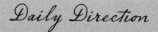

Daily Direction

Who is the author whose work ignited your own Burning Desire to Write? Pull out your old books by that author and read them again, and allow that to inspire you.

Genre Counselor

If you'd like, you can have a counselor for each genre that you write in: nonfiction, the various genres of fiction (suspense, thriller, romance, western, and so forth), articles, essays, poetry, and so on. Each counselor's responsibility will lie in the area of that particular genre and help you achieve success in that writing subject.

Working with Your Counselors

Once you've identified the categories that you need a counselor for and have chosen an image to represent each of the different counselors, you're ready to take the next steps.

Write It Down

Record in your journal each category of counselor you create and a brief description of the image you will use. For example, if you want to write comedy and need an idea counselor, you might choose to use an image of Mark Twain as your guide. Jot that down in your journal. If you are using your favorite author role-model as your plot counselor, record that. Do this until you have a complete list of counselors that make up your guidance team.

Sample Questions

The next step is to make a list of questions or problem areas that you will need your counselors help with. Below are some sample questions that you can pose to your various counselors. This is not an exhaustive list. You will want to formulate questions that relate to your unique situation. Your questions should be as specific as you can make them, especially if you need help with a particular problem area.

Sample Questions for a Daily Writing Counselor
- Daily writing counselor, what steps do I need to take to make writing part of my daily routine?
- Daily writing counselor, what I can do to avoid distractions to my daily writing habit?
- Daily writing counselor, how can I get my family's support so that I can write every day?

Sample Questions for an Idea Counselor
- Idea counselor, please give me a topic for an article for Magazine X that the editor will love.
- Idea counselor, please give me an idea for a hot new western romance series.
- Idea counselor, please give me an idea for a unique way to pitch my thriller novel to an agent.

Sample Questions for a Plot Counselor

- Plot counselor, please provide me with the next scene in my novel.
- Plot counselor, should I change the villain in my story to another character?
- Plot counselor, please show me the major points I should make in my essay.

Sample Questions for Career Guidance Counselor

- Career counselor, should I invest my time in learning to write fiction or nonfiction at this time?
- Career counselor, is Agent X a good match for me?
- Career counselor, is it a good idea for me to change genres?

Sample Questions for Genre Counselor

- Genre counselor, have I created a believable world for my sci-fi series?
- Genre counselor, is my biography of Napoleon Bonaparte historically accurate?
- Genre counselor, please provide me with a novel from my paranormal series.

As you can see, there are a wide range of questions you can ask your counselors. Create questions that are meaningful for you at this point in your career.

After you create your questions, pose them directly to your counselor, then pause and be open to receiving an answer. People experience the answer in different ways—you may "hear" your counselor say something, you may get a mental image in response, or you may get a feeling that you should take some action. It may take some practice to begin receiving answers but as with all subconscious mind communication, the more you practice the easier it becomes. After you receive an answer, thank your counselor for his or her wisdom and advice.

In the activity at the end of the chapter, you will be given the opportunity to use the guided meditation exercise on the CD to actually begin posing your questions to your counselors.

The Write Stuff

"One important thing I've learned is to surround myself with positive people. Encouragement is so important to me. My friends and family are always asking, 'Did you write this week?' If so, their approval is enough. If I didn't, they sling some wet noodles at me and tell me to get on it."

—Novelist Amber Leigh Williams

How to Use Your Counselors for Guidance

Once you begin the process of using the counselors for guidance, what you will find is that you can turn to them, in your mind, at any time for help and it will be readily forthcoming. For example, if you are having trouble getting to your desk one day, all it will take is turning in your mind to your daily writing counselor and asking for guidance, encouragement, support, or whatever you need at that moment to get to your desk. If you get stuck while writing your article, you can pause in your writing, turn to your idea counselor in your mind, and ask for help. As with all subconscious programming, this is a process that strengthens and builds the more you use it. Once you establish communication with your subconscious via your counselors, you will have advice and wisdom readily available any time you need it. It's as simple as that.

Counselor Conference

Another strategy for using your writing counselors to your advantage is to hold regular conferences with them. This process involves imagining yourself at a table with all of your Counselors seated around you. Again, have a list of prepared questions when you begin using this technique, but instead of posing your questions to just one counselor you pose them to all of them. You will likely get some interesting results; your idea counselor may have some insight into why you are not following your writing schedule, or your daily writing counselor may have comments to make about your current book's plot problems. This type of conference is always revealing, so you will want to have your journal nearby to record insights. This process can be done while in a guided relaxation state using the CD, or before you go to bed at night.

Daily Direction

Holding yourself accountable to your daily writing goal is one of the keys to writing success. You can do this by buddying up with another aspiring writer and sharing your daily word count goals. At the end of the week, check in with each other and hold each other accountable for having met the daily goal.

Have Regular Consultation

It's a good idea to set aside time to have a regular consultation with your counselors on a weekly basis, either individually or as a conference. Using the exercise on the CD, you can get into a relaxed state and communicate with each of your counselors about your writing habits and current projects. Once you are adept at this technique, you can simply get into a relaxed state, tune in to your counselors, and receive wisdom and advice. But in the beginning you should be sure to have a prepared list of questions to ask them to stimulate the subconscious mind communication process.

Activity: Talk to Your Writing Counselors

In your journal, record your categories of counselors and the images you have assigned to each one. Under each category, create questions based on the samples I provided earlier, but make these pertinent and meaningful to you and where you are in your writing life at this time.

Next, record your questions into your tape recorder or digital recorder. Repeat each question twice, and speak in a clear, slow voice.

Once you have recorded your questions, use the writing counselor track on the CD and play your questions when prompted. Have your journal nearby to record any insights or answers you receive once you come out of the meditation. Thank each of your counselors for any insight they may have given you during the exercise.

Live Your Life Write

Using various categories of writing counselors as a means of subconscious mind communication is a technique used by many successful people. A writing counselor gives your conscious mind a familiar image through which the subconscious mind can easily get guidance and wisdom to you. Remember:

- Create a writing counselor for every category of writing you want help in: daily writing habits, plot development, idea generation, career guidance, genre advice, and any others you may need.
- Communicate with your writing counselors on a daily basis using pre-formulated questions until you are adept at the process. Then you can communicate with your counselors easily at any point in the day.
- Be open to receiving the answers in a variety of forms, either "hearing" them or getting gut feelings, flashes of insight, or the sense that you should take some action.
- Remember to thank your counselors each time you communicate with them. Expressing gratitude strengthens the bridge between your conscious and subconscious minds.

Chapter 15

Slowly but Surely: Gradual Exposure

GRADUAL EXPOSURE IS A PSYCHOLOGICAL TECHNIQUE that allows you to take actions toward your daily and long-term writing goals little by little. It's a way to get your feet wet. These small actions build on each other over time and form habits such as daily writing, taking baby steps toward your big goals, and overcoming fear to take actions that will lead to the results you are seeking. The nice thing about using this tool is that you phase elements of the craft of writing and the writing life into your day-to-day routine. These are habits that strengthen over time. It's like steeping a bag of tea; the longer you leave the teabag in the water, the stronger the tea will become. In a similar fashion, the more you practice with the gradual exposure technique of incorporating the image of a successful writer into your thought-feeling-behavior cycle, the more successful your results will be. As you form the habit of daily writing and work on your writing goals on a regular basis, your chances for success, however you define it, improve dramatically; you will become a writer—slowly but surely.

The Process of Gradual Exposure for Writers

Gradual exposure helps you use the thought-feeling-behavior cycle to inch yourself along toward your goal of bringing the craft of writing into your daily life. This technique is particularly helpful in areas where you have resistance to writing or fear taking some action that is required to attain the success you desire.

For instance, let's say that you want to break into national travel magazines, but you fear putting together and sending out a query letter. This fear can stem from any number of things: lack of self-confidence, not feeling like you have time to properly research your subject matter, fear that you will get the assignment and won't be able to complete it, and so forth. Using gradual exposure, you would outline tiny baby steps, or what I call *micro-steps*, to achieve the goal of sending out a query letter to a national travel magazine. These micro-steps are best taken in small increments, such as one a day for one week.

The Write Stuff

"It's all been a series of sequential steps so far: writing the draft, editing that draft, querying agents, beginning work on a contracted trilogy, and so forth."

—Novelist Leslie Tentler

One Task Per Day for Seven Days

In this example, using the gradual exposure technique, on day one you would identify a national travel magazine to query. On day two you would identify your topic. On day three you would spend a set amount of time researching your topic. On day four you would draft the letter. On day five you would edit the letter.

On day six you would create a label for the envelope and put a stamp on it. On day seven you would mail the letter.

For additional impact, you can add visualization to your gradual exposure techniques in order to program your subconscious mind to help you reach these micro-steps. Depending on which area of mailing out a query letter to a national travel magazine was giving you the most trouble, you can target that area for success using your subconscious. If you are most concerned about your ability to research the topic, you can get into a relaxed state and visualize yourself finding reams of research on your subject. If mailing the query letter is giving you the cold sweats, visualize yourself going to the mailbox, smiling and full of confidence in your abilities, and dropping the letter in the slot. If you fear getting the assignment, imagine yourself turning in a competent, well-written article that your editor will love.

Using the technique of gradual exposure is an effective way to overcome all of those issues. It allows you to move gradually out of your comfort zone and take calculated risks. As you work to take steps outside your comfort zone, your comfort zone expands. You become more and more at ease with taking the steps necessary to reach a goal, and soon you are accomplishing things that a short time ago you were unable to for whatever reason.

You can also use gradual exposure to incrementally complete tasks related to the milestones on your Vision of Success *Plus*. Completing tasks in small micro-steps that accumulate and lead to the completion of big goals is a tried and true method for achieving outcomes.

Make Writing a Daily Habit

Bringing the craft of writing into your daily life is an area where the technique of gradual exposure excels. By using micro-steps, you can, in a short period of time, begin to entrench the habit of daily writing into your routine. Let's look at some different ways that you can use the technique of gradual exposure to attain writing success in various areas and then walk through the process of gradual exposure for an area of your choice.

"How Can I Write Today?"

Not feeling like writing is the downfall of many aspiring writers. Feeling inspired to write or feeling like the muse is sitting on your shoulder is the ideal condition to write, but it's rarely the reality. Successful writers sit down and write no matter how they feel and, more times than not, the act of writing brings the muse and the inspiration, not the other way around. Or, sometimes, writing is put on the back burner when other things crop up. The best of intentions to sit down and write fall by the wayside when distractions rear their heads.

To use gradual exposure to make daily writing a habit, ask "How can I write today?" Instead of dwelling on all the reasons why you can't write, or how much you don't feel like writing, turn the direction of your thoughts to a positive track. This changes your feelings toward writing from ones of dread to ones of anticipation, and your actions will follow.

Asking "How can I write today?" is a strategy that successful author Mary Buckham uses frequently. "The more you train yourself to write the more you write," she explains. "I am very careful about the types of questions I ask myself. Instead of, 'Why don't I feel like writing?'—which presupposes there is an option and sets up my mind to supply a logical justification to stay stuck—I ask 'How can I write fifteen pages instead of ten in my allotted writing time?' or 'How can I have fun with my writing today?' Questions like that set me up to expect to write, and to write more and in a positive way."

Asking yourself "How can I write today?" sets up the expectation that you *will* write. If an unforeseen obligation has cropped up, figure out how you can write while tending to the obligation, or before it or after it. Even if you only write one paragraph, you still wrote.

To use the one-task-per-day-for-one-week method of gradual exposure, ask yourself the question "How can I write today?" and each day, increase the amount of time or the number of pages you plan to write. So on day one, you might write one paragraph or two hundred words. On day two, ask yourself how you can write two paragraphs and 400 words. By day seven, you should strive to write seven paragraphs or 1,400 words, which is a healthy amount of daily writing for any writer! Of course this will vary depending on your individual needs, goals, and lifestyle. But the key here is to take some small action each day for a week and try to enhance the action each day until you reach your goal.

Daily Direction

To bring more writing time into your day to day routine, try this experiment: set an egg timer for ten minutes and write during that time. The next day, set the timer for twenty minutes. The third day set the timer for thirty minutes. Do this for seven days and you will be writing for seventy minutes.

Stack Up Finished Pages

Back in the days when writers used typewriters instead of word processors, one of the most gratifying tasks was to pile up the finished pages by the side of the desk and watch the height of that pile grow daily. This is a form of gradual exposure to a finished manuscript. As you watch the pages pile up, it motivates you to complete the work-in-progress. Even if you use a word processor, you can use this method of gradual exposure by printing out your pages when you're done and stacking them beside your computer.

To use the one-task-per-day-for-one-week method, you might start out typing a half a page. Day two you might strive to finish that page. Day three, write a full page. Day four might be to write two pages. By day seven, you might be writing up to five pages a day and stacking those beside your computer. Again, the micro-steps will vary depending on your individual goals and lifestyle.

Write Wherever You Are and No Matter What You're Doing

Life is so busy these days that it is sometimes difficult to see how to form the habit of daily writing when you first begin to write. One way to build writing into your daily routine is to keep your work-in-progress with you at all times, then seize any and every free moment to write down a scene, jot down ideas, or edit your current manuscript.

Novelist Barbara O'Neal did this in the beginning of her career, when she struggled to find time to write while working a job and tending to family obligations. Notice how she also weaved in the technique of positive thinking through the use of her bulletin board (described in Chapter 6). "I wrote as a regular practice, even if the time invested was an hour three times a week while the boys watched TV," she says. "I took a notebook to work and scribbled a page or two here and there. The finished pages encouraged me. I collected any positive feedback an editor wrote and put it on my bulletin board, which was right in the middle of the living room."

You can do the same thing. Keep your notebook with you at all times and increase the number of writing opportunities you seize each day. To use the one-task-per-day-for-one-week method, you might try to write in the morning while having coffee. Day two your micro-step might be to write on your lunch break from work. Day three the micro-step might be to write in the evening while your dinner cooks. By day seven, you will be writing during all of your breaks and during naturally free times of your day. Many a book has been written in this manner.

The Write Stuff

"For me to fall in love with a story requires me to put in a certain amount of time at the computer. That gets me thinking about it through the rest of the day and dreaming of it at night."

—Novelist Harley Jane Kozak

Set Week-By-Week Writing Goals

Your goal is to bring writing into your daily routine by writing every day. However, sometimes the demands of daily life may prevent you from sitting down at your desk every single day. When that problem arises, you can use the technique of gradual exposure by focusing on a weekly writing goal instead of a daily one. You would simply stretch out the one-task-per-day method to one task per week for a period of seven weeks. Here is how successful author Amber Leigh Williams does it. "Instead of day-by-day word-count goals, I think week-by-week," she says. "Then if something comes up on one day of the week, I can readjust my word count for the remaining days of the week to make it up for it. This way I don't have to punish myself or feel guilty about not meeting that day's word count. For me, a week-by-week word count is much more plausible."

If a week-by-week goal is a good way for you to bring the craft of writing into your life, you can accomplish it this way: week one, set a word-count goal, say 500 words. Increase that word count to 1,000 for week two. Week three's word count goal might be 1,500. And so on, until you reach week seven, which by then your weekly word-count goal might be as many as 3,500 words for the week. Adjust this goal up or down according to your own milestones and lifestyle.

Expand Your Writing Repertoire

Gradual exposure is an excellent tool to use when you want to expand your writing into other genres. When novelist Nancy Martin wanted to move from writing category romance to mysteries, she felt too intimidated by the intricacies of plotting a mystery to actually try writing one. So, over the course of several years, Martin applied herself to learning about mysteries and how they are constructed while she continued to write romance novels for a living.

Learning a new skill such as writing in a different genre is probably not something that you can do in a week. However, the technique of gradual exposure still applies. You break the steps down into micro-steps; first you might read three or four novels in the genre you want to write in over the course of a month or two. Next you might outline them to see how the author structured them; that might take several weeks. Next you spend several weeks looking for similarities in structure, plot formatting, character development, story arc, and so forth. Finally you draft your own new genre novel and create an outline for it based on your studies.

The key with using gradual exposure with any area of writing is that you break the big steps down into their smallest action steps. That's what makes it gradual exposure. You are *gradually exposing* yourself to each new, unfamiliar step in a way that makes it less scary, more approachable, and more doable.

Daily Direction
Set a goal to complete a short story that has seven scenes. Using the process of gradual exposure, write one scene per day for seven days, but each day, increase the word count of that scene by 100 words. At the end of the week, you will have the draft of a short story.

Generate More Writing Output

Successful authors give a lot of thought to how they can get more writing done in the same amount of time by using gradual exposure. Over time they push themselves to write more and more and increase their output. "Originally I started with the goal of writing one or two books a year," says Cynthia Eden. "But as I became a full-time writer, those goals changed. I wanted to write more, to do more. Last year, I wrote four novels and one novella."

You can follow in successful writers' footsteps by using gradual exposure to increase your daily writing output. From personal experience, I can tell you that pushing yourself to write more words or pages on a consistent basis has a lasting effect on your attitude toward writing. You start to hold yourself to that higher output standard and hence increase how often you write so that you can keep reaching that standard. Striving to generate more writing output is a good way to bring writing into your daily routine because you will be motivated to produce that higher amount.

To use the one-task-per-day-for-one-week method, try doubling your word-count goal each day. So if you start at 100 words on day one, on day two you want to write 200 words. On day three, you double to 400 words. On day four, you double to 800 words. And so on, until by day seven you will be writing 6,400 words in one day. That is a lot of words by any standard, and you can always back off to a lower, more reachable word-count goal if that figure is too high for your lifestyle. However, after doing this, it is unlikely that you will be satisfied with only writing 100 words per day ever again.

Gradual Exposure for Networking Purposes

Associating with other writers is a part of the process of becoming an author. You learn from other authors, published or not, and you receive support from and provide support to each other. Networking can be done at conferences, at workshops, and through writing organizations and critique groups.

Many writers are naturally introverted people, so becoming an outgoing personality in order to make connections with other authors can be a painful process. But it doesn't have to be. Novelist Lori Foster provides some insight into her experience with gradual exposure and how speaking in front of aspiring authors is now a rewarding experience for her. "I used to be painfully shy," she says, "but now, not so much. These days I actually enjoy speaking to big crowds, as long as they're crowds who are interested in hearing me. I can share mistakes I've made in the hopes that others can avoid them. I can share feelings I had so that others might better understand them when they're faced with the same emotional upheavals. And I can share advice, given from experience."

You may not have any plans to speak in front of groups of aspiring authors any time soon, but the principles of gradual exposure still apply. It's important to make connections with other writers, agents, and editors who will help you achieve your Vision of Success. The connections you make through writing venues will support you in the years to come as you work your milestones, just as it does now for author Harley Jane Kozak. "Most things worth doing entail risk, and it's especially true in artistic endeavors," she says. "I have a lot of friends engaged in similar pursuits that I call on for advice, pep talks, cheerleading, and then I return the favor when it's their turn."

As an aspiring author, you can create similar avenues of support for yourself through networking. Some of the ways you can use gradual exposure to help get your feet wet in the writing network scene include:

- Joining a writing group and volunteering to be a part of their conference committee.
- Attending writing conferences and planning to meet at least two new people at each one. Sit with people you don't know at lunch and strike up a conversation with your neighbor. Starting out with the question, "What do you write?" is a good ice breaker.
- Joining an online writing critique group. You can locate these through most writing organizations in your area.
- Participating in National Novel Writing Month (NaNo-WriMo) and look for a writing buddy.
- Writing and practicing your three-minute elevator pitch so that when you meet with an agent or editor at a conference, you have it down and won't get tongue-tied.

Taking these steps to immerse yourself in the world of writers will enhance your writing efforts back home, increase your chances of success, and inspire you to write. Writing conferences are where people find answers to the many questions that aspiring authors have when they first begin this process. Author Debra Webb found this out before she was career published. "I had been writing stories since I was a little kid," she says. "Finally one day I decided to get serious and actually attempt to get published. I had no plan. I just started looking for the right people to talk to and the right places to submit to. After about three years I made the right connection."

If you prefer to use the one-task-per-day-for-one-week method, break the steps down into micro-steps. For instance, you might try looking for writing organizations on day one. On day two, you read about the organization. On day three, you send an e-mail inquiry. By day seven you should have plans to attend their next meeting.

Submit Your Work

The first time you submit your work to an agent or editor for consideration—either a contest or a query letter or a synopsis or a book proposal—can be a humbling experience. Sometimes it feels like you are mailing out your very heart and soul to be held under scrutiny. It's understandable why this process intimidates many aspiring writers. Your first acceptance letter can be just as intimidating—if not more. You may begin to wonder if you will actually be able to write the piece you queried about.

All writers go through this, and that feeling of fear never totally goes away. Each new development in the writing career brings with it a certain amount of anxiety. "Learning to give a workshop. Learning to talk in front of people. Writing my first query. Writing my first synopsis. All of these steps were necessary baby steps to growing a career in publishing," says author Mary Buckham. "What I learned was to stop being afraid of doing the unknown and start looking at opportunities to push my comfort zone, which is all fear is about."

Usually, just getting started is half the battle, and the process of gradual exposure can help. Learning to submit work and then deal with the rejection or the acceptance of it is something you must tackle if you want to be a writer.

The process of gradual exposure to writing every day, submitting your work, and networking at conferences to make needed connections opens up to you a whole world of opportunities, opportunities that often take you in new and exciting directions as author Annette Fix found. "Those opportunities have taken me on paths I never would've planned to take," she says. "Because of my work on a women's writing website, I was asked to speak at a national writer's conference. It was completely unexpected and not something I had set a goal to do, but I enjoyed the experience so much that I've taken on more national and regional speaking gigs and have branched out to teach in-person and online workshops based on those lectures."

Activity: Applying Gradual Exposure

Choose an area where you have difficulty bringing writing into your life. This can be in any of the categories we discussed in this chapter such as writing every day, submitting your work, generating more output, expanding your repertoire, making connections, and so on. Or it can be an area not identified here where you would like to see small, incremental improvement.

Identify your problem area on a new page of your journal. Then break that overall goal down into seven micro-steps. Assign each micro-step to a day of the upcoming week. Write the task down on your calendar if necessary to remind you to do it. At the end of the week, record your results as well as any insights you had as a result of using gradual exposure to overcome the problem.

Live Your Life Write

Gradual exposure is a time-tested psychological method that allows you to slowly but surely make progress toward a goal that has given you trouble in the past. Its applications are broad and flexible and allow you to stretch out of your comfort zone to try new things with writing. When using gradual exposure, remember:

- Break a large task down into seven micro-steps.
- Assign one task per day for seven days.
- Complete each task daily.

Chapter 16

Twenty-One

Day

Program

HERE, WE WILL DISCUSS A WAY FOR YOU TO APPLY ALL OF THE CONCEPTS presented in the book over a three-week period to help you bring the craft of writing more into your daily life, and to help you lay the groundwork for maintaining your enthusiasm, motivation, and dedication so that you can achieve long-term success.

For convenience's sake, I will be suggesting a format for using the techniques presented in the book over a one- to three-day period, but feel free to adjust the time frames so that they suit your individual needs. The important thing will be to complete the exercises and actively use them within the twenty-one day time frame in order to build these habits into your routine. You may have been working the exercises in the book as you read along; if so, please take this opportunity to review, tweak, or even re-do them according to the time frames below in order to capitalize on the twenty-one day time frame.

Days One and Two: Invite Your Craft into Your Daily Life

The first objective in the program is to bring more writing into your day to day life. You cannot become a successful writer without paying attention to your writing life on a regular basis. It's also important that you begin focusing on your thought-feeling-behavior cycle and how this helps or hinders your efforts.

On days one through two, focus on becoming an observer of your own behavior. Do you write every day? Do you write every week? Why or why not? Focus on your thoughts and how they affect your feelings and behaviors toward writing. Change any negative thoughts that affect your writing efforts to positive ones. This is the activity in Chapter 1. This is the foundation exercise because you must determine where you are right now in order to make necessary changes.

The Write Stuff

"I think a successful writer needs to ask herself some hard questions on a regular basis. What's your writing goal? Then, what kind of book do you really want to write? When you've answered the first two questions, you are prepared to face the third: Does the book you want to write enable you to achieve your first goal?"

—Novelist Nancy Martin

Day Three: Define Your Writer Self-Image

On day three, give some thought to your Writer Self-Image by looking at what you want to accomplish through your writing. Write down your goals, then list the reasons why you want to achieve these goals. Publication does not have to be your goal in order to achieve success as a writer. Success comes in many forms. Define your *why*. This will be where your motivation, dedication, and enthusiasm lie and represent the core of your Writer Self-Image. Then write out your Writer Self-Image statements and post them where you can see them every day. This is the second activity in Chapter 2.

Days Four and Five: Create Your Dream

Over the next two days, give thought to your overall Vision of Success. This is your Big Dream, your ideal writing life. Think big and dream big here. Then, create a Vision of Success *Plus*, which is your vision with milestones at one-, three-, five-, ten-, and twenty-year markers. Use the exercise on the CD to help you with this exercise. You may also use the process of backward chaining to help you create milestones. Focus on how your milestones can bring writing into your daily life. Remember that daily actions are important to create success. What actions do you need to take every day in order to achieve your writing dreams? This is the activity in Chapter 3.

Day Six: Set Your Milestones

Capitalize on your thought-feeling-behavior cycle to start making progress on your Vision of Success *Plus* milestones. Review or make a list of the thoughts, feelings, and behaviors that you need to cultivate to reach your milestones. Next, identify the element of the thought-feeling-behavior cycle that is the strongest for you—in other words, is it easier for you to act first and feel later? Or do you need to have positive thoughts first in order to make positive behavior changes? Everyone has an element that is their strongpoint, so choose yours. Then list the thoughts, feelings, and behaviors you need in order to reach your milestones. This activity can be found in Chapter 4.

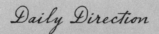
Daily Direction
Keep your whys, or the reasons you want to
achieve your writing goals, by your computer as an
endless source of inspiration and motivation
to write every day.

Day Seven: Take Control of Your Thought-Feeling-Behavior Cycle

Create and actively begin using your "I" statements from Chapter 5 to foster a sense of empowerment for your writing success and take control of your thought-feeling-behavior cycle.

Days Eight and Nine: Develop a Writer's Mind-Set

Now that you have brought writing more into your daily life, it's time to strengthen that foundation by developing a writer mind-set that will enhance your Writer Self-Image. On days eleven through thirteen, you will tackle self-doubt by writing an author biography, similar to those you see on book jackets, and then reading this biography to yourself as you look in the mirror. You may also recite your Writer Self-Image statements and "I" statements while looking in the mirror. You can find more details on these activities in Chapters 6 and 7.

Days Ten and Eleven: Pick Your Role-Models

Continue the process of strengthening your Writer Self-Image by choosing either a role-model or a composite role-model and using the process of Image Incorporation to absorb your role-model's success-oriented traits into your own lifestyle. Use the guided meditation on the CD to help you with the Image Incorporation process. For maximum effectiveness, continue the Image Incorporation activity every day for the remainder of the program. Chapters 8 and 9 teach you about role-modeling and Image Incorporation.

Day Twelve: *Act As If*

Begin *acting as if* you are the successful writer you want to be. Capitalize on your Image Incorporation and role-modeling experiences to mentally become the writer you wish to be. This activity can be found in Chapter 10.

The Write Stuff

"I would never have finished that first book and submitted it if I had not been hooked deeply by writing."

—Bestselling author Dianna Love

Day Thirteen: Your Key Writer Self-Image Words

Define your Key Writer Self-Image Words. These are power words taken from your goals, your Vision of Success, your milestones, and your biography. These words should be repeated mentally and out loud as often as possible as you move through your day. These words reinforce your Writer Self-Image, keep your thought-feeling-behavior cycle on a positive track, program your subconscious mind for writing success, and keep your conscious mind focused on daily writing. This is the activity in Chapter 11.

Day Fourteen: Write Your Script

Identify your Writer Script and theme using the activity and rewrite any problem areas into a positive script. Recite the positive script in front of the mirror several times. Create Positive Self-Talk questions as a means of staying focused on your writing goals every day. Chapters 12 and 13 cover this material.

Day Fifteen: Meet Your Writing Counselors!

Create your Writing Counselors. This is an image that the conscious mind can recognize that allows for ease of subconscious mind communication. These Counselors may be Plot Counselors, Daily Writing Counselors, Genre Counselors, Career Guidance Counselors, and so on. Use the exercise on the CD to begin the process of communicating with your subconscious via Writing Counselors. Review Chapter 14 for more information on this activity.

Days Sixteen Through Twenty: Slowly But Surely

Identify those areas where you still need help bringing writing into your daily life and use the process of gradual exposure to create micro-steps to overcome problem areas. Create one micro-step per day for the next seven days. This activity is covered in Chapter 15.

Day Twenty-One: Review Your Program

Complete the gradual exposure micro-steps and re-assess. Review all of your exercises and record in your journal any insights you have gained over the three-week period. Make adjustments to your program as needed.

Live Your Life Write

Completing the activities and reviewing them as a whole gives you a solid foundation that will allow you to establish a solid Writer Self-Image, develop confidence as a writer, build a writer's mind-set, and create reasons for working toward your writing goals. Daily actions are important to achieving your Vision of Success and they will sustain your motivation, enthusiasm, and dedication to your craft for many years to come. Remember:

- If you did not complete the activities as you read along, take this opportunity to do so now.
- If you did complete the activities as you read along, take this opportunity to make any necessary adjustments to your program.
- Redo all the activities within a three-week period and record your insights in your journal.

Afterword

Your Living Write Toolbox

Congratulations! You have completed a program that will allow you to bring the craft of writing into your daily life and enhance your chances of success as a writer—however you define it. Now you have many tools in your toolbox that will allow you to become the writer you have always wanted to be. These tools include ways of developing a strong Writer Self-Image, increasing your self-confidence as a writer, overcoming doubt and fear, and incorporating the traits of your most admired writers into your own daily habits. You have ways to talk positively to yourself whenever you stumble on your journey toward your Vision of Success, and you have milestones to celebrate along the way. You understand the importance of the thought-feeling-behavior cycle and can now use this cycle to create your desired outcomes in your writing life.

I hope that these techniques help you find success as a writer. It has been a pleasure to bring you this book, and I thank you for reading it. Remember, there are many forms of success, and yours is within your grasp. I believe in you, and I believe in your success. Please write to me and let me know how these tools are helping you become a successful author. You can reach me at *Kelly@ KellyLStone.com*.

Until then, happy writing!

Author Biographies

Alan Bradley (*www.flaviadeluce.com*) received the Crime Writers' Association Debut Dagger Award for *The Sweetness at the Bottom of the Pie*, as well as the first Saskatchewan Writers Guild Award for Children's Literature. He is the author of many short stories, children's stories, newspaper columns, and the memoir *The Shoebox Bible*.

Amber Leigh Williams (*www.amberleighwilliams.com*) is the author of *Denied Origin, Forever Amore*, and the *Wayback Texas* series.

Anna Hackett (*www.annahackettbooks.com*) is an Australian-born author who writes for Harlequin Silhouette Nocturne Bites. Her latest release is *Hunter's Surrender*.

Annette Fix (*www.annettefix.com*) is a freelance writer, speaker, and author of *The Break-Up Diet: A Memoir*. She is the former senior editor of *WOW! WomenOnWriting*, an online magazine written by, for, and about women in the publishing industry.

Barbara O'Neal (*www.barbaraoneal.com*) is the bestselling author *The Lost Recipe for Happiness* and *The Secret of Everything*.

CJ Lyons's (*www.cjlyons.net*) medical suspense novel, *Lifelines*, debuted from Berkley in March 2008 and became a national bestseller. The second in the Angels of Mercy series, *Warning Signs*, was released in January 2009 and the third, *Urgent Care*, in October 2009.

Cynthia Eden (*www.cynthiaeden.com*) is an award-winning novelist of paranormal romance and romantic suspense. Since beginning her writing career five years ago, she has contracted fifteen novels and ten novellas.

Debra Webb (*www.debrawebb.com*) wrote her first story at age nine and her first romance at thirteen. She is the bestselling author of spine-tingling romantic suspense novels for St. Martin's Press and Harlequin Intrigue. Her latest release is *Everywhere She Turns*.

Dianna Love (*www.authordiannalove.com*) is the *New York Times* bestselling author of *Phantom in the Night* and other novels. She is the winner of the RITA award and the Daphne du Maurier award. She teaches writing workshops based on her book, *Break Into Fiction: 11 Steps to Building a Story That Sells*, coauthored with Mary Buckham.

Harley Jane Kozak's (*www.harleyjanekozak.com*) debut novel, *Dating Dead Men*, won the Agatha, Anthony, and Macavity awards. Its sequel was *Dating Is Murder*, followed by *Dead Ex* and *A Date You Can't Refuse*. Her short prose has appeared in *Ms. Magazine, Soap Opera Digest, The Sun*, and the anthologies *Mystery Muses, This is Chick Lit*, and *Crimes by Moonlight*.

Leslie Tentler's novel, *Midnight Caller*, is the first in a trilogy being published by Mira Books. *Midnight Caller* will be available in February 2011.

Lori Foster (*www.lorifoster.com*) is a Waldenbooks, Borders, *USA Today, Publishers Weekly*, and *New York Times* bestselling author. She has published through a variety of houses, including Kensington, St. Martin's, Harlequin, Silhouette, and Samhain. Her latest release is *The Watson Brothers*.

Mary Buckham (*www.MaryBuckham.com*) is an award-winning romantic-suspense author who, before becoming published in book-length fiction, sold hundreds of articles to local, regional, and national publications as a freelance author. She's the coauthor of *Break Into Fiction: 11 Steps to Building a Story That Sells* and the novels *Invisible Recruit* and *The Makeover Mission*.

Nancy Martin (*www.nancymartinmysteries.com*) is the author of forty-eight pop fiction novels in mystery, suspense, historical, and romance genres. She was nominated for the Agatha Award for Best First Mystery of 2002, and her novel *How to Murder a Millionaire* won the RT award for Best First Mystery. Her latest release is *Our Lady of Immaculate Deception*.

Bibliography

Brown, Christina M. and Kimble, Charles E. "Personal, Interpersonal, and Situational Influences on Behavioral Self-Handicapping." *The Journal of Social Psychology*, 2009, 149 (6), 609–626.

Fresco, David M., Moore, Michael T., Walt, Lisa, and Craig-head, Linda W. "Self-Administered Optimism Training: Mechanisms of Change in a Minimally Supervised Psychoeducational Intervention." *Journal of Cognitive Psychotherapy: An International Quarterly*, 2009, 23 (4), 350–367.

Hill, Napoleon. *The Law of Success in Sixteen Lessons*. (Chatsworth, CA: Wilshire Book Company, 2000).

Hill, Napoleon. *You Can Work Your Own Miracles*. (New York, NY: The Random House Publishing Group, 1971).

King, Stephen. *On Writing*. (New York, NY: Pocket, 2002).

Koller, Alice. *The Stations of Solitude*. (New York, NY: Bantam Books, 1990).

Murphy, Joseph. *The Power of Your Subconscious Mind*. (New York, NY: Bantam Books, 2000).

Tracey, Brian. *Goals! How to Get Everything You Want Faster Than You Ever Thought Possible*. (San Francisco, CA: Berrett-Koehler Publishers, Inc., 2003, 2004).

Index

About the Authors

Kelly L. Stone (book author) is a licensed mental health counselor who started a successful writing career while working a full-time job. Her first book for writers, *Time to Write: More Than 100 Professional Writers Reveal How to Fit Writing Into Your Busy Life*, reveals the time management secrets of 104 professional writers and was nominated for the American Society of Journalists and Authors 2008 Outstanding Book of the Year award. *Thinking Write: The Secret to Freeing Your Creative Mind* describes how to use the power of your subconscious mind for maximum creativity. Kelly lives with her family in Florida. E-mail Kelly at *Kelly@KellyLStone.com* or visit her website: *www.KellyLStone.com*.

R. Michael Stone (CD author and performer) received his BA with Honors from the University of Florida in 1974 and his MS from Auburn University in 1976. For over thirty-three years, he has worked as a counselor developing subconscious communication and subconscious programming techniques. He is the creator of *The Unlearn Smoking Success System*™. Contact him at *michaelstone@unlearnsmoking.com* or visit his website: *www.rmichaelstone.com*.

SOFTWARE LICENSE AGREEMENT

YOU SHOULD CAREFULLY READ THE FOLLOWING TERMS AND CONDITIONS BEFORE USING THIS SOFTWARE PROD-UCT. INSTALLING AND USING THIS PRODUCT INDICATES YOUR ACCEPTANCE OF THESE CONDITIONS. IF YOU DO NOT AGREE WITH THESE TERMS AND CONDITIONS, DO NOT INSTALL THE SOFTWARE AND RETURN THIS PACKAGE PROMPTLY FOR A FULL REFUND.

1. Grant of License
This software package is protected under United States copyright law and international treaty. You are hereby entitled to one copy of the enclosed software and are allowed by law to make one backup copy or to copy the contents of the disks onto a single hard disk and keep the originals as your backup or archival copy. United States copyright law pro-hibits you from making a copy of this software for use on any computer other than your own computer. United States copyright law also prohibits you from copying any written material included in this software package without first obtaining the permission of F+W Media, Inc.

2. Restrictions
You, the end-user, are hereby prohibited from the following: You may not rent or lease the Software or make copies to rent or lease for profit or for any other purpose. You may not disassemble or reverse compile for the purposes of reverse engineering the Software. You may not modify or adapt the Software or documentation in whole or in part, including, but not limited to, translating or creating derivative works.

3. Transfer
You may transfer the Software to another person, provided that (a) you transfer all of the Software and documentation to the same transferee; (b) you do not retain any copies; and (c) the transferee is informed of and agrees to the terms and conditions of this Agreement.

4. Termination
This Agreement and your license to use the Software can be terminated without notice if you fail to comply with any of the provisions set forth in this Agreement. Upon termination of this Agreement, you promise to destroy all copies of the software including backup or archival copies as well as any documentation associated with the Software. All disclaim-ers of warranties and limitation of liability set forth in this Agreement shall survive any termination of this Agreement.

5. Limited Warranty
F+W Media, Inc. warrants that the Software will perform according to the manual and other written materials accom-panying the Software for a period of 30 days from the date of receipt. F+W Media, Inc. does not accept responsibility for any malfunctioning computer hardware or any incompatibilities with existing or new computer hardware technology.

6. Customer Remedies
F+W Media, Inc.'s entire liability and your exclusive remedy shall be, at the option of F+W Media, Inc., either refund of your purchase price or repair and/or replacement of Software that does not meet this Limited Warranty. Proof of purchase shall be required. This Limited Warranty will be voided if Software failure was caused by abuse, neglect, accident or misapplication. All replacement Software will be warranted based on the remainder of the warranty or the full 30 days, whichever is shorter and will be subject to the terms of the Agreement.

7. No Other Warranties
F+W MEDIA, INC., TO THE FULLEST EXTENT OF THE LAW, DISCLAIMS ALL OTHER WARRANTIES, OTHER THAN THE LIMITED WARRANTY IN PARAGRAPH 5, EITHER EXPRESS OR IMPLIED, ASSOCIATED WITH ITS SOFTWARE, INCLUDING BUT NOT LIMITED TO IMPLIED WARRANTIES OF MERCHANTABILITY AND FITNESS FOR A PARTICU-LAR PURPOSE, WITH REGARD TO THE SOFTWARE AND ITS ACCOMPANYING WRITTEN MATERIALS. THIS LIMITED WARRANTY GIVES YOU SPECIFIC LEGAL RIGHTS. DEPENDING UPON WHERE THIS SOFTWARE WAS PURCHASED, YOU MAY HAVE OTHER RIGHTS.

8. Limitations on Remedies
TO THE MAXIMUM EXTENT PERMITTED BY LAW, F+W MEDIA, INC. SHALL NOT BE HELD LIABLE FOR ANY DAM-AGES WHATSOEVER, INCLUDING WITHOUT LIMITATION, ANY LOSS FROM PERSONAL INJURY, LOSS OF BUSINESS PROFITS, BUSINESS INTERRUPTION, BUSINESS INFORMATION OR ANY OTHER PECUNIARY LOSS ARISING OUT OF THE USE OF THIS SOFTWARE. This applies even if F+W Media, Inc. has been advised of the possibility of such dam-ages. F+W Media, Inc.'s entire liability under any provision of this agreement shall be limited to the amount actually paid by you for the Software. Because some states may not allow for this type of limitation of liability, the above limita-tion may not apply to you. THE WARRANTY AND REMEDIES SET FORTH ABOVE ARE EXCLUSIVE AND IN LIEU OF ALL OTHERS, ORAL OR WRITTEN, EXPRESS OR IMPLIED. No F+W Media, Inc. dealer, distributor, agent, or employee is authorized to make any modification or addition to the warranty.

9. General
This Agreement shall be governed by the laws of the United States of America and the Commonwealth of Massachu-setts. If you have any questions concerning this Agreement, contact F+W Media, Inc., via Adams Media at 508-427-7100. Or write to us at: Adams Media, a division of F+W Media, Inc., 57 Littlefield Street, Avon, MA 02322.